EVERYTHING EVER AFTER

(Confessions of a Family Man)

MICHAEL PICARELLA

Illustrated by F. M. Hansen

MHP

LOS ANGELES   SANTA BARBARA

EVERYTHING EVER AFTER

A Muse Harbor Publishing Book

PUBLISHING HISTORY

Muse Harbor Publishing paperback edition published May 2014.

Published by Muse Harbor Publishing, LLC,
Los Angeles, California
Santa Barbara, California

Cover and Illustrations by F.M. Hansen.

Interior Design by Typeflow

ISBN 978-1-61264-145-4

Visit Muse Harbor Publishing at

www.museharbor.com

Happiness is a state of mind. It's just according to the way you look at things. So I think happiness is contentment but it doesn't mean you have to have wealth.

—Walt Disney—

This book is dedicated to my family, especially my wife, Lisa, and our son, Robert, who let me exploit them in the stories you're about to read.

I also dedicate this to my parents and my in-laws for showing me how it's done.

CONTENTS

Acknowledgements

THERE ARE SO MANY PEOPLE I WISH TO ACKNOWL-
edge, but I'm going to miss a bunch of them by accident.

I wish to thank my family (Lisa Picarella, Robert
Picarella, Joseph Picarella, Roberta and Jack Maley, Lorie
and John Deering, Tom and Michelle Picarella, Ross Pool,
Kim Pool and beyond) for providing much inspiration
and much more support than anyone could ever ask for.
My poor wife alone has had to read too many of my sto-
ries under such tough deadlines, even when she was sick.
Thank you.

This book would not have been possible without Lisa
Rule and John Loesing at The Acorn Newspapers, who
suggested I write a humor column for the paper. I have to
thank Steven Holt for first giving me a job as a reporter and
features writer at the *Acorn*. Thanks to him and John, my
newspaper mentors, I'm a way more betterer writer than
when I started. Thank you to Jim Rule, Andy McGinnis

and all the editors and copy editors (some past and some still present) at the five Acorn publications, including Daniel Wolowicz, Steve Carlson, Kyle Jorrey, Scott Tittrington, Idie Emery, Leslie Haukoos and Carol Pond. And thank you to the rest of my Acorn family, who put out the best newspapers in the world every week.

I should also mention Jeanne Pedersen from the *Acorn*. Not only did she make my writing better and tell me lies about how much she liked my work, she also suggested my column to her former publisher at The Signal. Thank you Jay Harn for listening to Jeanne and pushing to run my stories. I'm also indebted to Lila Littlejohn of The Signal, who gave my column star treatment at the paper.

Then there's Alicia Napolitan who read so many of my stories while she was at work and gave such important feedback. There are my biggest fans (next to my mom), Scott and Diane Camper, Barbara and Ken Widdis, and the barbers at Angelo's Barber Shop. There are all those people out there who read my column regularly, whom I consider the greatest readers ever. I give a special thanks to the readers who took the time to write me letters — you made so many bad days great.

Going way back, I owe my favorite English teacher from Rancho Cotate High School, Mr. Steffy, a debt of gratitude. In college it was my first screenwriting professor Stewart Lindh who got me excited about writing, and it was another writing professor, Skip Press, who got me thinking about how to make money with a keyboard.

Of course, this book would not be in your hands without Dave and Eileen Workman at Muse Harbor Publishing. Not only did they and their amazing team make the publishing process a terrific experience for me, but they also didn't need me to hard sell the project to them. They liked me. They really liked me.

I owe so much to F.M. Hansen for making this book look so cool. Thanks for the amazing illustrations.

Wait, there's more. There are friends, writers, filmmakers, artists, comedians and a bunch of other people whom have left indelible marks. Here's a short list of some of those people in no particular order: Matthew Skala, Evan Ball, Shane Clark, Jack Perez, Stuart Diamond, Chris Erskine, Robert McBrearty, Ryan and Naomi Staley, Jared Adams, Nick Meadows, Diane Franklin, Robert McKee, Mike Marino, Ron Miller — I can really do this for a few pages …

Finally, I want to thank Adele Pool, who is no longer with us. She proved you can aim for the Moon. And hit your mark.

UTURBiA

An Introduction by the Author

A HIGH SCHOOL GRADUATION CEREMONY WITH ITS "Congratulations," "You did it," "Nothing can stop us now," and other false ideas about the transition from adolescence to adulthood leads many graduates into thinking that college and a successful life are quick to follow.

Act now and you'll get more than just a degree, the ad says. *The dean of the institution of your choice will throw in the American Dream at no extra cost.*

The scene takes place during the mid-1990s in a small chain restaurant at a tiny corner table, featuring three of my friends and me, munching on a healthy slice of our own ideas about the American Dream.

A brand-new high school graduate, I was young, energized and hopeful; at the head of the table with a plate full of goals.

On a typical night, my friends and I would scrape together what change we had for a small plate of cold mozzarella sticks. Someone always treated the group to a round of on-the-house waters. On this big night of success, however, none of us had a dime to spare, but I was young, energized and hopeful, so I splurged and put the four-piece mozz' sticks on my tab.

While we waited for our banquet, I eagerly discussed my plans for a winning life. College was the answer. It's where I'd attain the training I needed to earn a career. It's also where I'd find the perfect woman — I knew this because I took the campus tour and examined the stock. "Mighty fine pickings," I told my friends.

Once I received my degree, I explained, my school would place me in the working world using the successful job placement program they had advertised out front in neon, and as my career picked up steam, my relationship with Mrs. She's The One would get serious.

"And then comes the baby in the baby carriage," one of my friends at the end of the table offered with a side of sarcasm. We called this friend Feet because he had a way of kicking you when you were down.

Not feeling down at all, I dismissed the offering and grabbed another helping of gullibility — the kitchen was all stocked up.

"You sound like you're giving one of those stupid graduation speeches at the ceremony today," Feet said to me, "with your five easy steps to the American Dream."

"So wait," said the goofy friend next to me, whom we called Perry, "you're getting married to someone you haven't even met yet?" To this day I can't remember how Perry got his nickname, let alone recall what his parents originally named him. My friends all laughed at Perry, but they were really chuckling at my expense, none of them with solid plans of their own.

"When it's his turn in line to buy a bride," Feet said, "he's gonna order the Number Two with legs, no nagging and a Coke. A few years after that, he'll be in the suburbs somewhere receiving catalogs by the baker's dozen when it comes time for offspring. He'll grab the baby booklet off the mantle underneath the wedding portrait, thumb through the options while sipping a cognac, and find the perfect baby. 'Just mark the box next to the child of choice,'" Feet announced in a salesman's voice, "'and in nine months your very own bundle o' joy will arrive.'"

"I think I'll pass on the extra helping of cynicism," I said. "I don't care if it is your number one special."

"Do you think life is gonna be that easy just because you finished high school?" asked the quiet one we all called Big Mouth. "Do we all really believe that high school graduation is that big of a deal? How would everyone feel if we didn't graduate?"

"You're right," I said. "Maybe it isn't such a big thing. That's because we live in a nice, safe area with good schools and lots of support. All we have to do is what we're told for 12 years of public education and, yes, high school graduation should be a cinch."

I sipped a glass of Do-I-really-know-what-I'm-talking-about? and continued. "All of us here were privileged to receive some scholarship money, and we're even more fortunate to have parents willing to fund — or take out student loans to fund — the rest of our college educations, should we choose to go that route. And once again, all we have to do is attend and absorb, and our futures are ours. We can build our own Suburban Utopias — our *Uturbias*, if you will."

By the end of the evening, I couldn't get my friends to swallow another bite of what I was feeding them. Feet kept stomping on my dreams, Perry thought I'd become goofier than he was and Big Mouth had came up with some other life mystery to ponder.

As we got older, my friends went their ways and I went mine. Sure, our paths crossed again. Sometimes they found me on the side of the road and helped with a jump-start. Sometimes I found them on the side of the road and probably made matters worse. After gobbling down those cold mozzarella sticks that night, separate ways we went, indeed.

I graduated college in the late '90s. In 2000, I married an amazing woman I'd met in school. (No, I didn't pick her up at a drive-thru window during some dorm party.) A couple years after that, my wife and I began the long process of buying a suburban castle of our own in a wonderful little town in Southern California, and we'd quickly filled our lives with the appropriate suburbanalia — bikes for neighborhood rides, extra sugar for our neighbors and, of course, wind chimes and a door knocker with the family name engraved into it.

Yup, life was good, but it certainly wasn't what I expected it to be. I didn't receive a complimentary career with my college degree; finding the perfect wife and getting her to marry me didn't mean I could stop working on the relationship; and building and maintaining my home was just as never-ending. Everything my friends told me on our graduation night was, well, wrong. But I was wrong, too.

I thought I could have my cake and eat it, too. I thought I could have heads *and* tails if I only worked hard.

My life education continued.

The birth of my son in July of 2003 brought more revelation and more surprise. Not that my son made life bad. Rather, quite the opposite. But I'd be lying if I told you life wasn't more complicated.

Nevertheless, I still felt I had a shot at that happy ending where all my dreams came true. No bite was more than I could chew.

In May of 2006, the publishers of the *Acorn* newspaper group in Southern California, who paid me for six years to report news and write feature stories, gave me the opportunity to write my own family humor column, which I named Family Men Don't Wear Name Brands.

With that column, I was able to document my experimentation with my own American Dream. I experienced many "fires in the kitchen," most of which showed up in story form in my column, twice a month in the five *Acorn* publications.

Just before the winter winds blew the 2007 calendar shut, the publishers of *The Signal* newspaper of Santa Clarita, CA, allotted me space in their paper for a similar column called "Picarella Family Report." Served hot every Friday for two years, my column spilled the contents of what was becoming my Uturbia.

And then I was broke.

When I was 34, the economy collapsed and my work slimmed down. My steady climb to cloud nine came to a halt. If I wanted to maintain the lifestyle my family was used to, I'd have to consider going back to the manual labor job I worked in high school; the job that supported me through college; the job I ecstatically left to earn my living as a small-time writer.

To some, going back to an old occupation meant failure. I didn't think that at all. But I considered every other remotely possible option anyway. I even looked into becoming the youngest crossing guard in the history of the profession. I just couldn't find work.

So I sold our cars, leased roller skates, got rid of the house and rented someone's closet. I was wearing the same clothes since Tuesday… of the previous month.

"Mike," my wife shouted. "You're daydreaming again."

I checked to make sure — yup, I was wearing clean clothes and we still had our house and cars.

Still, there was nothing more we could cut to make ends meet, no matter how hard we tried, and I didn't want to eat mozzarella sticks for the rest of my life. After much deliberation, my wife decided that I'd elect to go back to where I started, back to my first job — manual labor with low but at least steady pay. It was the right thing to do. It was the only thing to do.

While I filled out the online application, my son, who was seven at the time, tried to keep me in high spirits. He talked about the wife he was going to pick out when he grows up (he's a dreamer just like his dad).

"She's gonna have blonde hair," he said, "a pink shirt and jeans, and she's gonna wanna play trucks with me all the time."

By the time I submitted my application, I knew I was making the right decision. My family's interests were more important than anything else.

The next day, on the drive to the interview, I tried to wrap my teeth around the idea that maybe it's not possible to have "all of the above" in a multiple-choice scenario, no matter how hard you try. I walked into the place I'd long since left, and tried to accept those sights, sounds and smells that I swore I'd never have to take in again. I promised I'd never go back, that I'd keep moving forward. To go back would be to give up.

Maybe I wouldn't get the job.

I got the job.

My wife and son were thrilled when I announced the news. When I didn't share their hoorays, my wife said, "I thought you wanted this job."

Want the job?

I made the best of it. On my first day of work, I entered the building feeling positive. It's not like I was Tim Robbins's character in *The Shawshank Redemption* as he encountered prison. Then I heard the employees, like the prisoners of *Shawshank*, chanting at me, "Fresh fish … fresh fish … fresh fish!"

That was just my imagination.

When I clocked in, I heard my cell door slam closed. That was my reality — I was doomed, no longer the hopeful person I was following high school graduation.

After my first day back, friends and family, who knew I was down, tried to cheer me up.

"You weren't going anywhere before anyway."

"You gave your dream your best shot."

Even my wife said, "At least you *have* a job."

Yes, I had a job. My family could eat again. We could pay our bills, and we no longer owed anyone any money. But it seemed like something in me died. My failure was a reality.

On my way to work the next day, I said goodbye to my wife and son knowing I'd never return as the same person.

"It's been a lot of fun," I said in a man-going-to-the-chair kind of way. "I enjoyed the time we had together, and I'll cherish it forever."

Before I got into my car to leave, the woman I love gave me a big kiss and my little boy offered a picture he drew of me at my new job.

"It's for you, Daddy," he said. "I'm so proud of you."

There was some perspective.

Each day after, I went to work feeling better about my choice. Sure, I went backward with the move, but maybe I'd been on the wrong path toward my goals all along. The American Dream can be annoying like that.

Years ago in that chain restaurant with my friends and those cold mozzarella sticks, I imagined an existence I didn't achieve. Instead I did better.

Now I'm pleased to present the day's blue plate special, a single serving of stories about my continuing journey through life as a family man from the 'burbs. These stories come from both of my newspaper columns (some stories revised for this publication). They take place between my son's third year of life and his ninth, though they're organized thematically and are not in chronological order. From one story to the next, it might seem like I have a five-year-old son and a three-year-old son and a nine-year-old son. It's really the same kid.

I take on life's obstacles as Suburb Man, battling the *You can't have your cake and eat it, too* theory with great ability and amazing frustration.

Hey, at these prices, you can't expect choice steak and lobster for every meal.

So take a stool at the counter. Place your order for the American Dream of your choice. Here in Uturbia, the coffee pot is never empty. Bacon and eggs — and even those awful, but tasty mozzarella sticks — are served around the clock, and a fresh slice of apple pie is always on hand. Eat up. I did. And I'm relishing *everything* ever after.

— *Michael Picarella*

CHAPTER ONE

~~~~~~~~~~~~~~~~

Marriage

"I Do" Means a Lot of "You Don'ts"

I Can't Make Decisions

WIFE: So whaddaya want for dinner?

ME: Ummm —

WIFE: You wanna go out?

ME: Yeah. Sure.

WIFE: You decide. Where do you wanna go?

ME: Ooooh, let's go to Maria's Italian Deli. They've got that really good manicotti. And cannoli. That sounds good.

WIFE: But we just had Italian food two nights ago. Where else would you want to go?

ME: Let's go to Dave's, then.

WIFE: That's too fattening. What about Salt Creek Grill?

ME: That's too expensive. What about BJ's?

WIFE: We always go to BJ's.

ME: Well, where do you wanna go then?

WIFE: It's your decision.

ME: OK then. Everyone in the car. We're going to Maria's.

WIFE: I thought you didn't wanna go to Maria's.

ME: No, *you* didn't wanna go to Maria's.

WIFE: Can we go somewhere else? Anywhere but Italian food.

ME: OK, how about the Route 66 Grill?

WIFE: Isn't that kinda like Dave's?

ME: I guess it's somewhat like Dave's.

WIFE: How about Margarita's?

ME: Is that where you wanna go?

WIFE: It's your decision. Do you wanna go there?

3

ME: No, but if you wanna go there, then let's go.

WIFE: No — just pick where you wanna go.

ME: I did pick where I wanna go. You didn't like it. And you didn't like my second and third choices either. So you tell me where you wanna go.

WIFE: Are you mad at me?

ME: No, I'm just hungry, so choose where you wanna go, and let's go.

WIFE: I'm sorry — go ahead, you choose where you wanna go.

ME: OK, Maria's.

WIFE: Maybe we should just eat at home.

ME: Fine.

WIFE: What do you wanna have?

ME: Spaghetti.

WIFE: But we just had Italian food two nights ago.

ME: How about meat loaf?

WIFE: Kinda fattening, don't you think?

ME: Steak?

WIFE: Anything healthier?

ME: Pork chops?

WIFE: Hmmm —

ME: Chicken? Fish? Tacos —

WIFE: Which one do you want?

I went into the kitchen, got the cereal, the milk, bowls and spoons, and I put it on the table. I sat down, poured the cereal into a bowl, poured the milk, and I started eating. My wife and our son joined me.

WIFE: This was a good idea, sweetie. So whaddaya want for Christmas?

ME: I'll shop for myself.

— December 2009

The Big "B"

IT WAS TEN O'CLOCK ON A TUESDAY MORNING IN JULY. I was already eating lunch—a roast beef sandwich at Skip's Deli down on 11th Street. They made the best coleslaw at Skip's, and I made sure not to spill any of it on myself. I was wearing a leisure suit with a gold chain around my neck, with white athletic socks and white tennis shoes on my feet. I was everything a neighborhood kid ought to be, except I wasn't from the neighborhood. I was here to make a drop.

The Girl lived here. This was the kind of place where they spell "coffee" N-O N-A-M-E B-R-A-N-D-S, and if you suggested a chain store, they'd kill you.

The Girl and I first met at Barney's, a coffee joint a few doors down. We'd only dated for two months and within a week had already shared a roast beef sandwich at Skip's. We joked about other couples, how they'd come up with those ridiculous pet names for each other like Sugar Bub, Snooky Wookums and Baby Bunny Berry Pie. We promised that we'd never make up pet names for each other.

Until today. The Girl had gone too far—too far from home. She was on vacation at the other end of the country, visiting an aunt and uncle. Yeah, The Girl had gone too far, and I'd make her pay.

At 10:30 a.m., The Landlord of the building usually stepped out to take The Mutt for a walk—the kind of walk that means some poor homeowner would receive unsolicited lawn fertilization. Once The Landlord left for that walk, she'd leave the four-unit complex vacant.

I'd use that time to slip into the building and into The Girl's apartment with keys I'd secretly duplicated at the Do-It Center, and I'd make the drop. Afterward, I'd high tail it back over to Skip's before my slice of warm apple pie lost its steam.

It was to be an easy job, like finding trouble in Troublesville, only I'd be the trouble, and The Girl would find me — or rather she'd find my handiwork in her living room when she got back from her trip. You see, I'd created a giant looming…

Hold that thought. The Landlord just exited the building with The Mutt. They were early. It was 10:08 a.m., to be exact. She was making her way around the block, which meant I had about 20 minutes to get into the building, drop off The Package and get out before she returned.

I finished off my coleslaw, asked The Waitress to hold my table and the tab, and I made my way across the street to the apartment complex. I unlocked the main door with my duplicate key and propped it open, then I went to the second door on the right, unlocked it with my other duplicate, and propped that door open.

With speed and skill, I nonchalantly sprinted out of the building, down the walkway to my parked sedan across the street, and looked both ways before I pulled out the six-foot-tall…

Hold that thought. The Landlord and The Mutt were heading back to the building! There went my easy job. I was stuck, and my apple pie back at Skip's would surely get cold. I'd never get those doors closed before The Landlord reached the building entrance. She'd see me and wonder how I got a key, or she'd think I was a burglar and have me arrested. I could always tell her I knew The Girl. Perhaps she'd even seen me with her, but she'd never allow me in the building without The Girl's company.

I acted before I thought about what I was gonna do. I ducked out of view into a nearby bush and set off my car alarm, which produced the kind of noisy blast you might hear just before you die. It sent The Mutt, with The Land-lord in tow, into a mad dash in the opposite direction. I then made my move back into the building with The Package, and made the drop. I buttoned up the place, de-squawked my car alarm and was back at Skip's finishing my lunch when The Landlord and The Mutt returned, looking like deflated balloons. Success.

When The Girl returned from her trip, she found a giant looming six-foot-tall bumblebee — stinger and all — that I'd cut out from cardboard and painted. The insect's hands held a big paper sign with the words "Welcome Home, My Little Honey Bee" written on it. The Girl called and thanked me for the lovely and unexpected gesture. She even appreciated my ridiculous pet name humor.

Ever since then, The Girl — who I've come to call my wife — has never, ever, not even for a second, gone too far from me. She also expects unexpected gifts at unexpected times, all the time.

Such is my luck.

—*June 2008*

FAMILY NEWS IN BRIEF

WIFE GETS CHILLY DURING CAR RIDE HOME

During the ride home from dinner the other night, my wife reported that she felt cold; the first case of her being cold all summer, and a sign that summer is coming to an end. Goose bumps on her arms confirmed her chills. "I'm freezing," the lady of my life told me as we got onto the freeway. "Can you turn on the heater?" Experts advise those who, like my wife, get cold to wear warmer clothing such as pants (not shorts) and sweaters (not T-shirts). The same sources also don't recommend sandals when exposed to chilly climates.

WIFE HATES ZOMBIE MASK

At 1:42 p.m. on October 25th, at the local Halloween superstore, I strapped on a zombie mask and scared my wife into a stack of plastic black caldrons. "It's just a mask," I said as I helped her off the floor. According to my wife, she's been deathly afraid of zombies ever since seeing some zombie movie back in the 1980s. "The fact that my husband of eight years doesn't know I hate zombies is more of a problem than his little scare stunt at the Halloween store the other day," she said. In those eight years of marriage, I did happen to learn that my wife loves flowers. I bought her a few thousand roses following the "zombie" incident... and all is allegedly well.

R.E. POOL MEMORIAL SHELTER CLOSES

My father-in-law's cherished R.E. Pool Memorial Shelter for Downtrodden Husbands in Santa Clarita, which provided local support and outreach to downtrodden husbands, shut its doors yesterday, after eight years of service, due to a lack of participation and attendance. According to local wives, husbands have never been happier. "There's no need for such a ridiculous shelter," said one area wife, who wished to remain anonymous. Several other wives echoed the sentiment, and said their spouses would certainly agree. Husbands, however, weren't allowed to comment on the matter for this report.

Everyone Wants Our Babies

WHEN YOU'RE SINGLE, EVERYONE ASKS WHEN YOU'RE going to date. When you're in a serious relationship, they ask when you're going to get married. When you marry: "When are you gonna buy a house?" Then it's, "When are you gonna have a kid?" and "When are you gonna have another kid?" I imagine that being followed with, "When are you gonna retire?" Are people gonna eventually ask when we're gonna die?

I'm married, my wife and I are paying to own a house, and we have a five-year-old boy. Everyone asks when my wife and I are going to have another kid.

"It's so cruel to leave your son an only child," people tell us. They make us sound like we starve our child and beat him with a garden hose.

The other day at the grocery store, a stranger told my wife that she better have a second kid before our first turns six — or it'd be too late. Not waiting for any logical reason why it'd be too late, my wife came to me crying and forced the "Should we have another kid?" talk, a conversation we've had many times.

We'd discussed it at great length in the past, and our decision to stop at one child seemed final. Why some random person from the grocery store made my wife think again was beyond me.

Friends, family, co-workers and, yes, strangers, too, have had no problem asking why my wife and I haven't had another kid. At what point is someone so comfortable that he or she can ask when I'm going to impregnate my wife? That seems like an X-rated conversation to me.

Someone once asked me why my wife and I wouldn't give our son a brother or a sister. I told this individual that it wasn't that we were trying to torture our son with such a miserable and lonely life, but that in an attempt to provide a sibling for our son, like the good parents we obviously are not, we lost two babies and jeopardized my wife's life.

"Third time's a charm," this person said.

I found it difficult to respond to that, but eventually said, "Hey, if my wife can't make a baby, I'm gonna put her down like a suffering pet and find someone else who can give me offspring."

I don't think the lady liked that.

Another person tried to change my mind about having more kids, even though I hinted that I wasn't comfortable with the conversation. When I told the guy that my wife and I — both working parents — couldn't afford another kid, he joked, "You write a family column. Why not just have the second kid and write him off as a business expense?"

I told him, "I already write off my house, cars, wife, son and vacations for that very reason, and if I add one more write-off, the IRS will surely audit me."

The guy left the conversation thinking I actually write off my life since I write about it.

In reality, my wife and I have had trouble having a second child. At one point, we assumed it was fate's way of saying we shouldn't have another. That was two years ago, and my wife and I haven't had a change of mind — for financial reasons, fate reasons and, most importantly, for health reasons.

So, back to the other day when some stranger in the grocery store told my wife that she better have another kid before our five-year-old turns six. My wife said she felt "selfish" for not giving our boy a companion. She said our son would be "lonely." She said our son could become "more responsible" if he had a sibling to take care of. This, of course, was brought on by a total stranger.

Today our son has a companion thanks to his unselfish parents. He isn't lonely, and he's had to become more responsible. Yup, my wife and I bought our son a pet fish.

— *August 2008*

Gardener? For What?

LAST SUMMER, MY WIFE ASKED IF I THOUGHT WE needed a gardener to maintain our front and back yards. My answer was a big "No!"

My dad took care of his yard work. My grandfather took care of his yard work. I'd be darned if someone else was going to do my yard work. I'm a Picarella man. I'll do my own work, thank you very much. I told my wife all of this, and then I said, "I have spoken, and that's that," which doesn't really mean much.

So my wife and I spent another three hours arguing about whether or not I should give up the landscaping duties at our home. From a bystander's perspective, I might've looked like a big dummy, fighting to do manual labor around the yard, which was especially dumb since the matter had nothing to do with the cost of a landscaper. We could afford one.

My wife pointed out that I hadn't even mowed the lawn in over three weeks when it should've been done on a weekly basis. I had to admit, the landscaping looked bad, but I'd been busy at work and just didn't have the energy or time to break out the lawnmower and gardening tools and spend half my weekend maintaining the place. That's how I lost the argument with my wife.

We got a landscaper the following week, and I have to admit, it was nice not having to do the work. I was able to spend more time with my family, I could rest after long days of work during the week … life was great!

And then my wife said the following:

"Doesn't the grass look greener and more lush than ever before?"

"What?" I asked. "No, it doesn't look greener or more lush than before. What are you saying?"

"I'm not criticizing you," she said.

"I'm not taking it as criticism," I lied. "I'm just answering your question. So, again, no, I don't think the grass looks any better than before."

I knew then that I never should have agreed to hire a gardener. Now my wife had one more reason why she could do without me. I needed to protect my job as a husband, not terminate it.

So, in September, we got rid of the gardener. I became useful again. And I'm a "real" Picarella man again, like my dad and grandfather, doing the yard again.

After firing the gardener, I spent that first weekend — the entire weekend — working on the front and back yards, and I must say that our landscaping never looked so glorious, so rich, so green and so lush. I was very proud of the work. My wife even recognized the visual splendor of the place.

The next week, I spent a little less time on the yard.

I skipped the following week's yard duties altogether since I was out of town. Once I got home, I didn't make up the work. And I didn't do it the following week either.

This continued until we got a letter from our homeowners association regarding a lack of yard maintenance. I was a bit embarrassed. My wife was upset.

Today, the landscaping looks great again — better than ever. And my wife is very happy.

I must say, it's good to have the gardener back.

— May 2008

BITS FROM THE 'BURBS

BETWEEN YOU AND ME

Nothings often mean so much more than *somethings*.

SAME OL' SAME

I'm reinventing myself. Already, my wife's telling me I'm not the man she married.

FOR THE RECORD

My wife and I have a major problem — we can't agree on which TV programs to delete off our DVR so we can have the space to record a show for our son, who's at a birthday party for the day. We have two hours before this program begins. Our kid really wants to see this thing. So we have to make some cuts — her shows or mine. Let the unfair assessments of my shows begin.

I'M A DUMMY

I stuffed newspaper in my clothes, put on a monster mask, propped myself up in a chair in the living room and passed myself off as a Halloween dummy. My wife — who was in on the gag — brought our son in for a look. "Oooooh, look at that scary monster," my wife said to our boy. "That's a dummy," the kid replied. "There's newspaper sticking out of the sleeves." Before I could scare my son into a coma, he gave me a good hard kick to test the dummy's durability. "Yup," my wife said, "that's definitely a dummy."

Smugglin' Ain't Easy

My six-year-old son and I are sitting in the car out in front of the house. I open a bag of chocolate chip cookies—one of our favorite treats, second only to M&Ms. I let the sweet aroma fill the car.

ME: You want some of these delicious cookies?

MY SON: Yeah!

ME: Then you gotta help me sneak 'em into the house without Mommy catching us. You help me do that, and you can have three whole cookies. How's that sound?

MY SON: You gotta be kidding, right, Daddy? Whaddaya think I am — a baggage handler? What'd I do for you on Halloween, when I handed over those Milky Way bars? What was that — a game of Candyland or somethin'?

ME: No kid of mine is gonna talk to me like that. I don't have to give you any cookies at all. I could've had Grandpa call Mommy on the phone to distract her while I snuck these cookies inside.

MY SON: So why didn't you? And who are you calling a kid? I'm six years old. I'll be six-and-a-half in a few months.

ME: Oh, so you're a big shot now, huh? You think you can make it in the big world all by yourself?

MY SON: You're kidding, right?

ME: OK, big shot. You're so big. There's a bag of M&Ms I've got stashed in my desk. Pure milk chocolate. I want you to sneak these cookies into the house all by yourself, and if you're as big of a big shot as you say you are, get these cookies into my bottom desk drawer without Mommy catching you. You do that, and that bag of M&Ms in my desk is yours. Do you know how to handle Mommy?

MY SON: Sure. But it's gonna cost you more than a bag of M&Ms and three cookies. Sneaking sweets into the house is no duck walk anymore. Mommy's like the Navy. She's got EC2 Hawkeyes with satellite tracking. She sees everything. And that's 'cause she's serious about eating healthy. So I want the M&Ms and I also want half the cookies in that bag — not just three.

ME: You've got guts making demands like that.

MY SON: In this world, Daddy, you gotta have guts. When you got guts, you get the power. And when you got the power, you get the sweets. Me? I just want what's coming to me.

ME: And what's coming to you, son?

MY SON: The world, Daddy, and all the cookies and candy in it.

I close the bag of cookies and drop it into my son's lap. I step out of the car.

ME: Meet me in your room in ten minutes. That's when you'll get your M&Ms and your cookies. But if Mommy catches you, you won't see another treat 'til high school.
MY SON: I'm scared.

I leave the kid in the car and wander into the house. He isn't far behind with the cookies.

MY WIFE: Where's our son?
ME: I dunno.

The kid enters, cookies in his hands.

MY WIFE: Where'd you get those cookies?

I wonder what the kid is up to, cookies out in the open. His idea of smuggling is different than mine.

MY SON: Daddy gave me the cookies.

I can't figure the kid's strategy, but he's got me fooled for sure.

MY SON: Daddy wanted me to sneak these into the house. He also has a big bag of M&Ms in his desk.

And this is the nightmare I have, just before I decide not to buy cookies at the store. I pick up a gallon of milk and a book of stamps — the only items I'm supposed to get. And I head home.
— August 2009

Val-ANT-ine's Day

I'm GUILTY — I HAVEN'T DONE ANYTHING REALLY thoughtful for my wife in a long time.

On the Sunday before Valentine's Day, she woke up from another nightmare. She said that, in her bad dreams, I'm usually there, not doing anything really thoughtful for her.

"What?" I exclaimed. "I do really thoughtful things for you all the time."

I couldn't let her think I wasn't husbandly anymore. I went to my desk, got a pen and paper, and I listed a bunch of thoughtful things I could do for her, to be appropriately executed on Valentine's Day.

Meanwhile, my wife went to the kitchen to surprise our nine-year-old son and me with breakfast.

"Ant!" she shouted from the kitchen as she prepared the meal.

"What?" I asked. "We don't have an ant. Not in over ten years of living in this house."

"Well, it's here," my wife replied. "And here are another two…three…more."

I went to the kitchen to check it out. She was right. We had ants.

And even though we never had a reason to own ant spray, I kept some handy under the sink…for close encounters. I grabbed the can, sprayed the line of the pests.

"That looks like all of them," I said.

"That's not all," my wife said. "Because if we have a few, then we have more. And if we have more, then that *will* be all. This breakfast I'm making and all our food — you can kiss it goodbye."

Our son heard the commotion, came in, saw the ants, freaked out. He grabbed a bottle of glass cleaner. "Let's rock!" he shouted, and then he lit up a line of crawlers near the toaster.

"No!" I yelled. "That glass cleaner's expensive. It's the kind that doesn't streak. Besides, we can't just keep wasting spray on surface ants. We gotta get poison, get them to bring it back to their nest."

"And how long's that gonna take, Daddy?" my son asked.

"I don't know," I admitted. "No more than seventeen minutes."

"Seventeen *minutes?*" he exclaimed. "This kitchen isn't gonna last seventeen *seconds.*"

He was right. I went back to spraying the ants with my ant spray. When the can was empty, I used the expensive glass cleaner. At least it didn't streak. Eventually, I ran out of that, too. And ants kept coming.

"That's it, game over," my son cried. "Game over."

"Are you finished?" I asked him.

"Maybe you're not up with current events," he sulked, "but we're getting killed here, pal."

The ants were now crawling on my wife and kid. My wife said I needed to think about her and our son, not just the kitchen.

Fine. I pulled my family out.

In the front yard, I discovered where the attackers were getting in. And I found what looked to be their nest and took it down with a few kicks.

"Someone's gonna have to go back in there and get the rest of them," my wife said.

"Oh yeah, sure, with those things running around?" my son bellyached. "You can count me out."

I volunteered. My wife looked at me in awe of my heroics.

"Look," she said, "We appreciate this. Now, I know we're all a little strung out of shape, but we just can't afford to let one of those things in our bedroom. I have enough problems sleeping as it is."

"Yeah, Daddy," our boy said. "Thanks for being so brave. Sorry I was being a little obnoxious back there."

As I turned my attention toward our dwelling, my wife told me to wait. She wanted to go with me.

"No, you're staying here," I said.

She gave me a kiss, said she loved me. I said I loved her, too.

Then I took her to the garage for some ant-killing gear: weed remover and wasp repellant, duct tape for body pick-up, paint masks to protect us from airborne poison. Before entering our house, I told my wife, "Remember: short, controlled bursts."

Our son kicked the door open for us. We went in with spray cans blazing. When I got to the wasp repellant, my wife's mask couldn't protect her. I gave her my mask then got back to killing crawlers.

I pulled apart the cabinets, got to the crawlers in the walls. When I looked back at my wife, she was struggling to get my mask on over hers. I helped. Her girlish grin was unmistakable.

In the end, we won. At night, my wife was still smiling. I asked, "You gonna be OK to dream?"

"Oh yeah," she said. I seemed to have proven my thoughtfulness for her. Yes!

Unfortunately, that didn't mean I was free from doing something really thoughtful for her on Valentine's Day. So I tucked her into bed. And I got back to that list of thoughtful things to do for her.

— February 2013

MORE FAMILY NEWS IN BRIEF

LITTLE TURKEY, LOTTA TURKEY, BIG TURKEY

If I suggested a big turkey for Thanksgiving, my wife would say, "What are you saying — that I'm big and need a big bird to fill my appetite?" So I suggested a small turkey. She said, "What are saying — that I'm big and need a small bird so I don't fill my appetite?" There was only one turkey in the room after that.

FATHER-IN-LAW EXPLAINS HEARING LOSS

My father-in-law recently realized that the deafness in his right ear might not have been the result of close gunfire while serving in the Vietnam War. He now attributes his hearing loss to something much closer to home. "I'm usually driving when my wife and I go anywhere," he said, "and she's usually on my starboard side, trying to improve my driving. Any husband knows how I really went deaf in my right ear." Asked if his wife could comment, my father-in-law said she wasn't available. That's his story and he's not letting her in on it.

"THERE'S NO PLACE TO SIT," SAYS WIFE

At about 4:30 p.m. on Wednesday, February 4th, my wife came home from a long day of work and said she couldn't go another night in search of a place to sit, that the constant mess in the living room was becoming a nuisance. "Every day," my wife said, "I come home tired, wanting to sit down, relax and watch TV, but I can't because my husband and five-year-old son have built a fort that takes up not some, but *all* of the living room. Or they've rearranged our couches to be a spaceship or a car or some Zapper 3000 machine." My son wouldn't comment on the matter. I apologized for any damages caused and promised that my wife, from that day forward, would always have a seat in the living room. The next day, as promised, my wife had a place to sit on the couch — right next to the starting point of the toy roller coaster my son and I built. Mommy could be the first person to place a marble on the track and watch it take a run down the sofa, over the coffee table, across the top of the TV and through a series of twists, turns and loops in the center of the room.

Good Listener

"DADDY, YOU'RE HOME!" SAYS MY NINE-YEAR-OLD SON with a hug before I can get in the house.

"Tell Daddy what kind of day you had," says my wife with a kiss before I can shut the door.

"I had a bad day, Daddy."

"He's not listening to me, Mike."

"I argued, too, Daddy."

"Mike, his arguing is getting out of control."

"I'm sorry, Mommy," the kid says.

"You've been saying sorry all day," says my wife. "I told you to clean your room. You said OK. Then you kept playing. How many times did I tell you to stop playing to clean your room?"

"Once."

"No. Three times."

"No. Twice."

"See, Mike, everything's an argument."

"No," the kid says.

"You just said 'once,' then you said 'twice.' I asked you to clean your room three times, did I not?"

"Yeah."

"So you just argued with me for no reason because now you agree that I told you three times."

"But I thought it was once and then I thought it was twice and now I know it was three times."

"Mike, do you wanna say something about this? This is the way it's been all day."

"No it wasn't," the kid says.

"Go to your room," my wife says to the kid.

"I'm sorry, Mommy."

"Go to your room," my wife repeats, setting my dinner on the table.

"How was your day at work? Better than my day here?"

"Mommy?" our kid calls from his room. "Can I tell you something?"

"Come here," she says.

"I'm sorry for being bad today."

"You can't treat me like this," she tells him. "You don't treat Daddy like this, do you? Daddy, does he treat you like this?"

"Yes," my son says matter-of-factly.

"You don't treat Daddy like this," my wife says to our son. "Now you're gonna argue about *that*?"

"No."

"But you're arguing."

"Sorry, Mommy," the kid says, leaving the first silence in the room since I got home.

"Is dinner good, Mike?"

"I helped make it, Daddy."

"So you didn't tell me how your day was," my wife says to me.

"Hey, Daddy," my kid cuts in, "Joey came over to play today."

"They got along really well," my wife says. "Oh, tell Daddy about the joke you guys made up."

"Oh, yeah. Mommy asked us what was next to the Salton Sea, and we said the Salton D."

"You know, Salton C, like the letter C," my wife says. "That's good, right?"

I don't answer my wife's question. I don't say a word. I sit in silence and finish my dinner.

My wife accuses me of not listening to her and our son. After a long day of not being heard, she'd hoped, she says, that *I'd* at least listen to her.

"I heard everything you said," I finally assure her. "Every word, every sentence, every event. Go on. Continue. I'm just listening."

"If you were listening," my wife tells me, "then what'd we say?"

"How can you accuse me of not listening?" I ask. I'm hurt. "You saw me listening. You saw me giving eye contact. You saw my facial expressions as I listened. Yet you want me to prove myself."

Yup, they want me to prove that I was listening.

"I'm a good listener," I say, and then I pause. "It's my memory that's not so good."

— *September 2012*

The Wife's Not a Fan of the Fan

MY WIFE HATES MY FAN.

It's a tall, two-speed oscillating fan that I use to keep cool at night while I sleep. My fan helps save energy and money by giving my air conditioner a rest, yet my wife can't stand the thing.

But before I make my wife out to have horns, a red tail and a pitchfork, I should give a little background on the fan. I can't lie — I don't use it just to keep cool. I've become addicted to the soothing humming sound it makes. So I fire it up each night, even on cold winter nights, for a sound that is to me what a lullaby is to babies.

The fan doesn't help my wife sleep at all. In fact, it annoys her. But she doesn't complain — not often anyway — because she took me for better and certainly for worse.

Last winter, my fan did my wife a favor and refused to turn on (probably from overuse). I threw a fit. A couple sucker punches to the motor made the thing start up. But in that moment, I realized I had a serious problem. I decided that I needed to kick my fan habit — right then.

Quitting was harder than I thought. I tried all sorts of methods to wean myself from the fan, but each night I needed that machine's pleasing noise to put me to sleep.

I bought one of those calming rain forest sound-effects CDs and looped it all night, hoping the sounds of crickets and birds in their native habitat would put me to sleep. Instead I tossed and turned and kung fu chopped the insects that I thought, by the sounds, were attacking me as I struggled to sleep.

I tried to quit the fan cold turkey. I asked my wife to hide the thing and keep it hidden no matter what I said, no matter how upset I got.

After one night without my sweet machine, I went into withdrawal, experiencing horrible mood swings. I needed my fan fix, but I couldn't find my fan.

I threatened my wife, telling her that if she didn't find the thing, I'd take her four-year-old son away from her.

She didn't give in. Instead, she suggested we play music at night as a substitute, even though she knows I hate listening to music while falling asleep.

On our first night as a married couple, my brand-new wife asked if playing music at night would bother me.

Still sedated by our "I dos" and wedding cake, I said, "If you wanna play music, please do, my love."

I hated the music. Even the songs I loved became total trash. My ears weren't meant to be a rock star's microphones while I slept. I soon learned that ever since my wife was a teenager, she needed music at night to sleep. I put up with her addiction for two years.

I finally suggested running a fan to kick the habit. I'd heard that the humming sounds could put anyone to sleep. So we bought a simple, affordable two-speed oscillating fan — the same fan I can't find now — and in a few nights, my wife didn't need the music anymore. A couple nights after that, she didn't even need the fan anymore. But that's when I got addicted.

Today, I'm in need of the magical sound those revolving blades make more than ever. The airflow is the cherry on top during these hot, humid nights. Still, my wife won't return what's rightfully mine.

So I agreed to use music at night to kick my fan habit. After a few torturous nights of that, my wife was good and hooked on music as a sleep agent again.

And then I hid the stereo from her, which tortured her.

Can you believe she still won't return my fan?

—July 2008

MORE BITS FROM THE 'BURBS

TURKEYS

My wife and I watched *A Charlie Brown Thanksgiving* with our six-year-old son. There's a really funny sequence with Snoopy and Woodstock struggling to get into a garage to find a table and some chairs for a Thanksgiving feast. The automatic garage door sends Snoopy into the air and through a basketball hoop. My wife and I were in hysterics. My wife laughed so hard, she rolled off the couch. Later in the sequence, a basketball bounces out of the garage with Snoopy attached. My wife and I couldn't hold it together. I laughed milk out of my nose. Next, Snoopy performs some fancy dribbling with the ball. Then he tosses the ball over to Woodstock so his little bird companion can show off, too. The ball flattens Woodstock. My wife and I burst into laughter and wouldn't stop. "Why doesn't he just get the table and chairs?" our son said, clearly annoyed. "He's not making any progress." Then the kid asked my wife to get off the floor and asked me to clean the milk off my face.

THAT'S COLD

My wife told me that Los Angeles doesn't have seasons. I told her she was wrong. Make no mistake — winter is here. I had to pull up the hood on my sweatshirt this morning.

Donuts

IT'S THE ULTIMATE BREAKFAST — DONUTS.

But is *ultimate* always good? Is all that glitters always gold?

When I was a kid, my family bought donuts every now and then. My dad made sure of that. I remember his favorite — Bavarian cream. Subsequently, Bavarian cream was my favorite, too.

Even when I got older (11 years old), when my friends and I spent the night in our fort during the summer, we'd wake up in the morning and get donuts. I always got the Bavarian cream. Yum.

My wife doesn't eat donuts, which means for the past 11 years since we've been married, I don't eat donuts either. Around ten o'clock last Sunday morning, however, my wife, our eight-year-old son and I passed a donut shop. A giant poster in the window advertising Bavarian cream-filled donuts called out to me.

"What are we gonna do for breakfast?" I asked my wife.

"We're not having donuts," she said, totally aware of what was going on in my mind.

"I know," I said. "But they're so good."

"But they're so bad," she replied.

We got stuck at a red light, and that donut advertisement taunted me.

"What're donuts?" our eight-year-old asked. Poor kid had no idea.

"We don't really have any breakfast food at home," I said to my wife. "And if we go shopping right now, we might as well just skip breakfast and do lunch."

Her look said it all. I didn't know I had it in me to so shamelessly manipulate her like that.

To the donut shop we went. My wife sat in the car.

"Just get six donuts," she said on our way out. "We don't need any leftovers."

The lady in the donut shop told my son and me that we could get a super baker's dozen (14 donuts) for the price of six donuts.

"But Mommy told us to only get six," the kid reminded me.

Six wasn't going to work. I needed at least four glazed donuts for myself. It's funny — no one wants to admit that glazed donuts are actually the best. They always say they're too plain. I used to claim that the Bavarian cream ruled the dozen, but I'd always grab a glazed first. And I'd always wrap up the "meal" with a glazed. I could no longer deny the power that that particular donut had over me. I was excited just thinking about it.

"We'll do the 14," I told Donut Lady. "And we'll start with six glazed." Then I looked to my son — "How many glazed ones do *you* want?"

Breakfast is the most important meal of the day. It sets the tone for the 24 hours to follow. When my son and I picked our super baker's dozen, I knew it was going to be a great day. For insurance, I ordered a somewhat healthy breakfast sandwich for my wife. And some fruit. That'd score me points.

After I paid, my son saw a glazed twist that was hiding in the back of the display case. He said the glazed twist was going to be his favorite donut once he tried it.

"It's too late now," I said. "It's not like we can switch 'em."

Donut Lady threw in two glazed twists for the kid — free of charge.

We left the store with the breakfast sandwich, the fruit and one big box of donuts.

"What happened to 'only six donuts'?" Mommy asked. She was actually upset, even though we got the six donuts like she requested…and ten more for the same price.

The entire morning was ruined. And it would most likely set the tone for the 24 hours to follow.

When we got home, my wife ate her breakfast sandwich and fruit. My son and I didn't touch our breakfast. I felt bad. I knew my wife didn't want to be tempted by all that sugary goodness in front of her.

When she was finished, I opened that big box. But, seeing the donuts, I couldn't eat a single one. The guilt hung over my head, then Mommy caught a glimpse of a rainbow-sprinkled donut.

"Can I have that one?" she asked.

That gave my son and me the OK to tear that box to shreds.

Finally, after all these years, I had the donut feast I'd so been wanting.

Four minutes and about 26 seconds later, after polishing off the last of the 16 donuts, I never wanted another donut again.

—January 2012

Distaste Test

THERE'S A PROBLEM IN MY MARRIAGE. MY WIFE demands that I taste her food when we go out to eat. It's like she's Al-Qaeda launching a war on my meal enjoyment.

Why can't we each just eat what we choose to order? If I wanted what she ordered, I would've ordered it.

With my decision to get a particular meal comes a taste palette I expect to savor. I can't simply add other flavors to the mix. That ruins the entire dining experience.

So maybe I'm a little hard on my wife when she pushes her food on me.

"Sure," I say, "I'll try it."

Maybe I'm not hard enough.

The other day, my wife suggested we try a new restaurant. That meant one thing: She'd want to sample. Wait, there's a second thing: She'd want me to sample, too. I hate that. When I set out to eat a meal, I budget the entire plate. I never eat over my budget (not often, anyway), and I want everything I've set out to eat. Giving even one bite of my meal away throws the whole calculation off balance.

I wasn't going to give in and go to this place to put up with the kind of meal blasphemy I've come to expect. I'd just have to tell my wife *no*, and demand that we go to a familiar place with no new dishes to try because we've had them all. I'd just have to be hard on her.

"Sure," I said, "I'll try it."

I marched into the new restaurant determined to eat only what I ordered. And I was going to eat all of my meal, too — share none of it.

I hated the place at first sight ... and smell. It was seafood. Even though both sides of my family come from Palermo, Sicily, a seafood town, and even though my last name, I'm told, has something to do with a fisher boat, I take offense to all things fishy. I can't even eat tuna fish. I knew I wouldn't want to try my wife's food. Heck, I wouldn't even want to try my own.

We sat down and I investigated the menu for anything edible. It was more like an interrogation.

I found one dish. Beef teriyaki. I could eat that.

Now, my wife knows I despise seafood, and that I've tried enough of it to know for sure that it's not for me. You name it, I've tried it — crab, lobster, sushi, salmon, shrimp. And I've had it prepared many different ways, even the way you make it. Sorry if I offend anyone, but it all stinks. With that in mind, it should've been easy to convince my wife to drop the whole taste-test thing.

"You wanna taste mine?" she asked.

"No," I said. "My palate is set up for beef teriyaki."

I hoped she wouldn't ask for a taste of mine because the servings were pathetic. If price had anything to do with portions, I should've had a month's worth of leftovers.

"Can I try some of yours?" my wife asked.

I couldn't tell her *no* even though I was planning on eating the exact amount of food on my plate. I couldn't be that hard on her. She's my love. I had to let her try some of my skimpy servings.

"Sure," I said. "You can try it."

I believe the word you're looking for is *spineless*.

I cut a small piece of my food for her to taste. The sample could've passed as a crumb. She asked for more. I gave her more — two crumbs. And I watched her cut a piece of her seafood for me to try. I wish she gave *me* crumbs. Instead, the portion she slid over looked more like a beached whale on my plate.

She delivered the whole "It doesn't have that fishy taste" speech that all fish pushers shamelessly apply to attract followers. Then she left me on my own and tried the sample I gave her. I jealously watched those morsels go down, morsels I'd budgeted for my personal intake.

My eyes fell back down to the fish on my plate. I took a bite. More like a lick. I swear I made contact.

Let's just say I inhaled my soda and all the water at the table in hopes of pushing that fishy taste it didn't have down into the pit of my stomach. Then I finished my micro meal and asked for the hefty check.

My wife suggested dessert. Enough was enough.

"Sure," I said, "I can try dessert."

Dessert was different, though. I could do the whole "trying thing" with dessert.

I tried everyone's dessert until all of it was gone. I guess it wasn't a terrible eating outing.

— December 2012

CHAPTER TWO

Parenting

Tales of Professional Amateurs

The Barber's Guinea Pig

My son, now three years old, has developed quite an imagination. I revel in the fact that he can wander into imaginary worlds or create imaginary games and beings. As a child, when lonely, I often relied on my imagination to pass time. It's a great tool. I fully encourage my son's ability to create things in his head.

My son loves the barbershop. He loves to sit up really high in the tall barber chair. He loves the scissors that go "cutting cutting," as he says. He loves the clippers that go "bzzzzzzzz." He loves the water bottle that goes "pssst, pssst." He loves the cash register and the "ding" it makes when the drawer opens. And of course, he loves when the barber gives him a lollipop to eat after the haircut.

It was only a matter of time before the barbershop would become a subject in his imagination.

For his birthday this year, among many gifts, my son received a lollipop that spins when you press a button on the handle. I suppose that's the lazy lollipop eater's way to lick a lollipop — with the mechanism, there's not much work to be done. The toy was a big hit with my son. He loved its sound and motion.

But once my son devoured the lollipop, he eagerly sought out new uses for the device. That lollipop spinner instantly became a barber's clippers. The toilet became the barber's chair, the sippy cup became the water bottle and a set of Bob the Builder toy pliers became the scissors. And I became the barber's customer.

All this was created from my son's wonderful imagination. Wow. I was so proud.

I played along with the kid. I became the imaginary barber's first patron and, after my imaginary haircut, I even gave my son some imaginary money, which he deposited into an imaginary cash register that went "ding."

But once I left the "barbershop," my son expected me to come back as his second, third, fourth and fifth haircuts. That's when I knew I was in trouble.

I should've known better. After all, a game of peek-a-boo could keep him entertained for three days straight.

The first 20 "haircuts" weren't so bad. But at 50, I'd had enough.

My scalp actually became raw from that lollipop spinner. I thought I felt blood dripping off my head after that 50th trim, but I later found out that the drop was only a bit of milk from the barber's water bottle — I mean sippy cup.

"OK, let's play a new game," I told my son.

"No, let me give you haircut," he replied.

"No, I'll give you ice cream. You want ice cream?"

"No, let me give you a haircut."

"You want a new toy car? How about one of those big jumpers for your room? You want Mommy and Daddy's room?"

"No, let me give you a haircut."

"How about a later bedtime? You wanna stay up all night and watch cartoons? Or maybe you want all my money? Here's my checking account number."

"No, let me give you a haircut."

For the record, I'm writing this column on my laptop computer during haircut No. 326.

—July 2006

Where Does My Son Get That?
Or:
The Tale of the Super Bike

I NOTICED THAT ONCE MY FOUR-YEAR-OLD SON started school, he started picking up bad habits.

Since beginning school, he now says "I can't," every time we ask him to do something. He'd never said that kind of thing before, and my wife and I always encouraged him to at least try.

Since beginning school, my son has said some horrible words that my wife and I never taught him. We never even whisper those words in his presence for fear he might hear and repeat.

And yes, since beginning school, my son has developed a problem with sharing, even though he always did fine with the neighborhood kids when my wife and I were around.

I think other kids are corrupting my child. I've talked to some of the parents at my son's school and asked what they thought. They're with me — they think the other kids at school are bad influences.

But what can you really do about that? You can't protect your children from all that's bad in the world. You have to teach them the difference between right and wrong, smart and dumb.

The other day, my son came home from school and said he had a question.

Great, what did he bring home now from the other kids at school?

He said he wanted to turn his bike into a motorcycle. He asked for a baseball card to attach to his bike so that when the wheels were turning, the spokes would flip the card repeatedly and create a motorcycle-like sound.

I never told my son about putting a baseball card in the spokes of a bike — like I used to do as a kid. I asked my wife if she taught our son about putting a baseball card in the spokes. She said she hadn't. So the obvious answer: my son is a genius.

"Wow, you're really inventive," I told my son. "I'm so proud of you."

I mounted a baseball card to my son's bike so that it would flip on the spokes when he rode the thing. Sure enough, it made a type of motorcycle sound. My son was having a blast, racing up and down the sidewalk as if he was going 200 miles per hour.

The next day, my son came home from school and said he wanted to put more cards in his spokes, and double up the cards as well, to make a louder motorcycle-like sound.

I never said anything to my son about beefing up the sound of his bike by doubling up cards and adding more cards along the wheel — like I used to do as a kid. I asked my wife if she told him about that. She said she hadn't. The obvious answer: my son is a genius.

So I doubled up the cards, added more along the wheel and, soon enough, my son was riding around on what he called his "super-fast motorcycle." He zipped up and down the sidewalk as if he was going 400 miles per hour.

The next day, my son came home from school and said he wanted to put a piece of thick plastic in the spokes of his bike to make his "super-fast motorcycle" supercharged. Wow, I never even thought of that as a kid. Great idea.

I asked my wife if she told him about putting a piece of thick plastic in his spokes to make his bike louder. She said she hadn't. Wow, my son really *is* a genius.

I found a piece of plastic that was being used as a partition between cars in one of my son's Matchbox car boxes. I mounted the plastic to my son's bike so that when the wheels turned, it'd flip along the spokes.

My son jumped onto his "supercharged, super-fast motorcycle" and took off down the sidewalk as fast as the speed of sound. And speaking of sound, the sound produced by the piece of plastic flipping against the spokes of my son's bike was like the sound of a dragster topped out in the red as it roars down a quarter-mile stretch of raceway.

Wow, that sounds really cool, I thought. *I wish I woulda thought of that when I was a...*

Just then I saw several spokes shoot out of the wheel of my son's bike. Yup, they shot out like the buttons on a guy's shirt ten sizes two small when the guy flexes his chest muscles. And then my son munched out in the bushes near Mr. O'Brien's house.

Now what kid at my son's school influenced him to put a piece of plastic in his spokes?

—*January 2008*

FAMILY NEWS IN BRIEF

DANCING WATER PRESENTATION A SHOWSTOPPER

Dancing water performed in what's now being hailed a stylish work of magic and intrigue. Last weekend, a packed crowd, including my wife and four-year-old son, stood around a man-made pond at a shopping center in Los Angeles and watched water squirt, spray and literally dance before us. "We basically have water jets, which are kinda like big squirt guns under the water, that shoot water out of the lake," said a janitor at the mall. "We program those big, high-tech water guns to move to whatever music the mall manager chooses to play." My son didn't want to leave the lake, citing the water display as "really, really, really neat." And so there we sat for three days watching water squirt all over the place to Neil Diamond hits and other super sounds of the type.

SON ANNOUNCES BIG LOSS IN THIRD QUARTER

My five-year-old son posted a big loss in the fiscal third quarter, after more than two dozen gold coins from his pirate-ship play set went missing during a routine vacuum clean-up in the living room earlier this month. The boy claims Mommy must've rolled over the coins and sucked them up. Mommy denies the accusation. "I opened up the vacuum bag and didn't find one toy," she said. My son sticks to his story, stating that the coins couldn't be anywhere but inside the vacuum. To assure Mommy and Daddy that this loss wouldn't become a trend, our boy said he'd protect his assets in the future by putting his toys back where they belong when he's done playing with them. We stakeholders — both Mommy and I — are happy with our son's new approach to toy management.

JET CRASHES, ONE MAN INJURED

A passenger jet carrying a reported 3,000 people from the Moon crashed in my living room yesterday morning. The damages were a nicked ear and a scraped cheek. "Our [5-year-old] son was flying his toy Southwest Airlines Boeing 737 over the Pergo Sea near the Love Seat Mountains when he encountered engine trouble," I told my wife when she asked about my face wounds. "The vessel went down — and it went down fast — crashing into my head at full speed." Asked if I was OK, I told her yes, the wounds would heal. But now my son needs a new jet because one of the wings broke off in Daddy's ear.

My Son's School Project

WHEN I WAS A KID, I ENTERED COUNTLESS GROCERY-store coloring contests, and colored my pictures with great skill and patience, my eye always on the first-place prize.

In school, when assigned a history day or science fair project, I worked with the same diligence for weeks — sometimes months — putting together amazing works of historic account and scientific ingenuity that were sure to earn me top honors.

The only thing that stood between first place and me: the parents of the kids in the competitions.

At six years old, I was quite an artistic force with my Crayola crayons, but I just couldn't compete with some of the parents who had backgrounds in fine art and commercial illustration. Nor could my middle school history-day movies that I produced on my home video camera compete with the "work of the kid" whose father worked for the local news station.

It just wasn't fair. Why did I have to do all my own work myself?

My five-year-old son is a kindergartener this year, and he's being asked to create projects that will, no doubt, compete with the "work of his classmates." Last month, my son's teacher asked the class to create posters about themselves, with pictures of them with their family, pets, etc. Before my son could get started, I sat him down for a little heart-to-heart.

"You're very talented," I told my son. "You're creative. You're artistic. You're inventive. But that doesn't matter... because I'm going to do your project for you."

I wasn't about to let my five-year-old lose to a 35-year-old.

I got started right away. I commissioned the artist who painted those popular 9–11 memorial posters back in '01 to create a moving piece of art that would capture the essence of my son. My wife thought I was crazy.

"You spent how much for just one picture?" she asked. She was right to be outraged. If I was going to spend that much money on the project, my son needed much more to show.

So I decided to produce a film as a companion piece to the poster, a three-part biopic dramatizing my son's early years. Lucky for me the Screen Actors Guild hadn't gone on strike, as they were threatening to do all summer. I was able to cast George Clooney to play me, Charlize Theron to play my wife and Nancy Cartwright (the voice of Bart Simpson) to voice the animated version of my son.

While shooting the big action sequence of my wife and me as we raced to the hospital for our son's birth, my wife pointed out that we didn't have a '68 Mustang Fastback GT390.

"We didn't race recklessly through the streets of San Francisco either," I said, "but we have to embellish our story a bit for this to be cinematic. Besides, we need good action sequences or all the money I laid out for the THX surround-sound system for the final presentation will go to waste."

It was when the school turned down my proposal to present a firework extravaganza as part of my son's poster project that my wife and son finally sat me down and asked if I thought I was going a little overboard.

"Overboard?" I asked. "It's not like I've got the Grave Digger monster truck crushing playground equipment at school. Although that'd be a good alternative to the firework display."

I immediately called Dennis Anderson's people over at Grave Digger Racing. My wife disconnected the phone before I could speak and, in a matter of minutes, masterfully talked me out of doing my son's project altogether.

Now I'm stuck with a film in production, I've got UPS out front with a truckload of George Lucas's THX audio equipment, I've got fireworks from all over the world brimming in my garage, and I'm the owner of a worthless half-painted masterpiece.

But my son is proud to present his class with his very own hand-drawn poster, and he's happy whether it's the best poster in class or the worst.

— October 2008

My 5-Year-Old and Skunks

MY SON: Hey Daddy, why do skunks stink?

Pause. I try to decide if I should just say, "Because," and end what could be a really long, pointless conversation … or if I should answer the question and educate my son.

ME: Well, you see, skunks don't stink. They spray a liquid that stinks.

MY SON: Why do they do that?

ME: They do that to anyone who looks dangerous.

MY SON: But I'm not dangerous.

ME: But the skunk doesn't know that.

MY SON: But I'd love the skunk if I saw him.

ME: Listen, if you ever see a skunk, walk away from it. Don't try to tell it you love it.

MY SON: But I won't hurt it.

ME: The skunk doesn't know that. The skunk just sees that you're big, and if you go toward it, it's gonna be afraid of you and it's gonna spray you. And then you'll stink, and it's gonna stink to wash all that stink off.

MY SON: But I don't want him to spray me. What if I just pet him?

ME: Don't ever pet a skunk. Don't ever even go near a skunk.

MY SON: But what if I see a skunk?

ME: Have you ever seen a skunk?

MY SON: In cartoons.

ME: Well, skunks are a lot nicer in cartoons than they are in real life.

MY SON: Are skunks bad guys in real life? Should we kill them?

ME: No, skunks aren't bad guys in real life. And no, we shouldn't try to kill *them*.

MY SON: But why do skunks have to spray their stink on people?

Pause. I try to decide if I should just say, "Because," and end this long, pointless conversation...or if I should answer the question and educate my son.

ME: Well, you see, every animal needs a way to protect itself from bigger and stronger animals. Since skunks are so small and can't really fight, they use their stink to make the other animals run away.

MY SON: So other animals are bad guys and we should kill them?

ME: No, other animals aren't bad guys. And no, we shouldn't kill any animals.

MY SON: But if other animals always wanna fight skunks, aren't the other animals the bad guys?

ME: They're not bad guys. In order to survive, all animals have to eat, and they usually eat smaller animals.

MY SON: Other animals sound like bad guys to me.

ME: Well, maybe they sound bad, but that's the way life works. Animals can't just go into a restaurant and order a lunch or a dinner. And they can't go grocery shopping and cook their own meals either. They have to hunt, beat and eat other living things.

MY SON: Why would another animal wanna eat a skunk if skunks smell so bad?

ME: Well, that's exactly why skunks stink. They don't want to get eaten.

MY SON: Sometimes when I go to the bathroom, I stink. Is that so other animals won't eat me?

ME: I never thought about it that way.

MY SON: When I see a skunk, I know what I'm gonna do.

ME: Walk away like I told you?

MY SON: No. I can make my stink like I do when I go to the bathroom before the skunk can make his stink on me. And then the skunk will run away and not even make his stink.

Pause. I try to decide if I should just say, "Good plan," and hope my son never bumps into a skunk ... or if I should respond truthfully and educate my son.

ME: Well, you see ... maybe it's time you ask Mommy about all this.

—*January 2009*

BITS FROM THE 'BURBS

RACE TO GET DRESSED

Getting a six-year-old dressed in a hurry can be a challenge. My son often gets distracted and can turn the task into an all-day event. To avoid being late to a particular engagement, I made the chore of getting dressed into a game. "Whoever gets dressed first wins," I said. And then came his rules: "OK, Daddy, if I get dressed first, then I'll run into your room. If you get dressed first, then you run into my room. If I run into your room, I win. If you run into my room, you win. If we both win, we'll crash into each other in the hallway..." After his 15-minute breakdown of the rules, and after a few "pauses" in the game so I could help him turn his socks inside out and tie his shoes, we successfully became late.

OVERHEARING

My nine-year-old son heard the woman's thick accent, and asked me if she was British. "No," I said. "She's from Texas."

CAM-PAIN-ING

My wife and I are feeling a bit tormented by our son who's constantly telling us he loves us. Don't get me wrong — we love the love. But he says he loves us every minute. My wife finally asked him, "When are you running for office?" He said, "Next year." As it turns out, he wants to be boss of the house in 2011.

Spanking Doesn't Work

I HAD TO SPANK MY FIVE-YEAR-OLD SON LAST WEEK-
end for bad behavior. He asked me, "Is that it?"

I don't like the idea of hitting my son. But I know it has
to be done in certain circumstances, especially when timeouts aren't working.

I now understand the saying, "This is gonna hurt me
more than it's gonna hurt you." Without a doubt, it really
hurts me to have to hurt my son. But I know he'll experience greater pain in the future if he's not disciplined.

My plan was to spank the kid just hard enough to sting,
but not hard enough to bruise. I gave him a gentle spanking,
but with enough force to make him think twice before doing
something bad again. When my spanking failed to startle
the boy, I took it up a notch, delivering a swat that I knew
would sting.

I hit him harder than I intended. I felt horribly guilty. I
asked if he was OK. He laughed. I gave him a time-out.

While my son was in his room thinking about his bad
behavior, I decided to do some spank tests on myself. I
smacked my bottom a few times to see what kind of pain I
was delivering. My son was right to laugh. I felt no pain at
all. So I applied a little more power. Still nothing.

I hit my hand, thinking that'd be more effective. Again, I
felt no pain. I did it harder. I've had breath hurt worse. I

guess our elders used wooden spoons, rulers and belts for a reason.

So I went to the kitchen, got a wooden spoon, and I practiced a few smacks on my left hand. Still, I felt no pain. I turned up the heat and, finally, I felt a little sting. But it wasn't enough to scare my kid into being good. I wound up and swung that wooden spoon again, this time like Barry Bonds swung a bat during the steroid years — WHAP!

My hand lit up like a bright red "Eat at Joe's" diner sign.

"Yeeeeeeowwwww!" I yelled.

I took a second swing, but with a little less power — WHOP!

"Yeeeeeeowwwww!" I yelled once more. By this time, I was developing bruises on my hand. So I switched to hitting my right hand. A few swats later, my right hand was bruised up, and I still couldn't deliver a painful smack that wouldn't leave marks.

I had to switch targets again. I took the wooden spoon and swung it at my behind.

"What are you doing?" my wife asked when she walked in on the scene. I froze while in mid-swing at my butt.

Our son yelled from his room, "He's spanking himself to see how hard he has to spank me so it hurts me just a little bit but not a lot."

"You're supposed to be thinking about your bad behavior," I yelled back to the kid. "No talking."

When I explained to my wife that I had to spank our child, she asked if it was necessary.

"It was necessary," I said. "The timeouts aren't working anymore."

Our boy chimed in from his room again, "Then why am I still in time-out?"

That question lead to an argument between my son and my wife. And that argument resulted in my wife spanking our boy. WHAP! WHOP!

"Is that it?" the kid asked Mommy when she was finished.

My wife said she was afraid to hit our child any harder for fear she'd leave marks and be reported for abuse.

"You're not gonna be reported for abuse," I said.

"I just want to be sure that if we hit him any harder, we won't bruise him," she said.

So she asked if I could continue banging myself around until I found the perfect spanking intensity for our son.

Now I can't walk.

— *May 2009*

No Playing, You Might Get Hurt

PARENTS, BE ADVISED: PLAYGROUNDS ARE DANGEROUS.

I'm the father of a five-year-old boy who loves playing at the playground, but my wife and I had to look for alternative ways to have fun, because a local kid allegedly fell off the monkey bars at a nearby park and broke his arm. Now the playground is under public scrutiny and, we're told, off limits.

"Can we go to a different park?" my son begged.

"I don't think so," I said, wanting to follow the rules. "Since all playground equipment is pretty much the same, I have to assume that all parks with playgrounds are dangerous."

The said park is said to have been around for nearly 20 years. In that time, according to neighbors, nobody has been seriously injured. But now we know — the place is a death trap.

"We don't need a playground to have fun," I told my kid. "We'll make our own fun."

We played bocce ball, rode bikes, tossed a baseball back and forth. My boy was having fun. And then he asked how much longer until we could have some *real* fun.

"Sorry, son," I said, "but we just can't play at the park until authorities say it's safe."

I asked some super parents what they were doing while the powers that be looked into the playground situation. They said they hadn't bothered bringing their kids to the park in years.

"We stick the kids in front of the TV or have them play video games," one parent told me. "It's more educational."

So my wife and I looked into it. We got one of those Leap Frog learning game units. Our boy became an instant fan. And the games were, indeed, educational.

"Look," I said to my wife. "He's having fun. And he's learning at the same time!"

We gave each other a high five.

Then we noticed something strange in our home. My wife and I found it difficult to walk down the halls without incurring an injury, and we couldn't hear each other speaking unless we screamed. This was because our kid was more hyper than ever, with more bounce in him than a Titleist golf ball that's zipped off the garage floor at 70 miles an hour. The boy was also louder than the demolition of a Las Vegas casino.

"I bet it's the game unit!" my wife yelled to me one afternoon in the kitchen.

We looked online to see if video games make kids hyper or unruly. Sure enough, we learned that, according to experts, video games are major sources behind juvenile violence for various reasons. Luckily, our kid hadn't joined any vicious gangs or killed anyone … yet.

"What're we gonna do now?" my son asked. "We can't play at the park or on anything that's taller than a park bench. And now I can't play video games?"

We set up the model train set, drove toy cars, played board games. It was a lot of fun.

"Now I know why they call them 'bored' games," my son said.

Evidently, my wife and I were the only ones having the fun. Our kid was antsy.

A neighbor told us that maybe our son had ADHD.

"He didn't just get ADHD overnight," I said to my wife afterward. "That's ridiculous. The kid is fine."

It took us less than five minutes to get to the pediatrician's office. And then it happened — while crossing the parking lot to the doctor's office, I stepped over a curb the wrong way and twisted my ankle.

"Yeow!" I yelled. "Stupid curb! That's dangerous."

"The curb's not dangerous," my wife said. "You weren't looking where you were going."

She was right. Then it occurred to me that maybe the park wasn't dangerous either. It also occurred to me that my son only became hyper after the playgrounds became off-limits.

"I bet he's hyper because we're keeping him cooped up," I said to my wife as I nursed my ankle in the parking lot. "He just wants to run around and play. That's what kids do."

We had a serious dilemma — we had a kid who wanted to let loose on some playground equipment, and we had authorities telling us that playgrounds were too dangerous.

So my wife and I made a decision — we told our kid, "Life's dangerous, be careful." And we enjoyed playtime at the park. Right after the doctor wrapped my ankle.

—July 2009

MORE FAMILY NEWS IN BRIEF

CONTRABAND FOUND IN KID'S BACKPACK

Last week, my wife and I caught our kindergartener smuggling contraband into his classroom. After giving him a hug and kiss goodbye, we noticed his backpack was half unzipped. "Right there in his backpack were three Matchbox cars, a plastic harmonica, about a dozen toy Army men and, worst of all, an extra bag of fruit snacks!" my wife said. Asked what he was trying to do with such goods, our son said, "I dunno." My wife and I confiscated the items and have been conducting routine searches of the boy's backpack since. "It's amazing what a kid packs in his bag," I told school authorities. "Key chains, random toy parts, even rocks. A boy's backpack is really his treasure chest." My boy has since been clean.

Kid Doesn't Need Bath

Late afternoon on Saturday, June 13th, in the Sacramento home belonging to my parents, my five-year-old son announced that he didn't need a bath, even though he'd spent the better part of the day playing in the sandbox at a nearby park. Sweltering weather conditions gave my wife reason to believe our kid got dirtier and sweatier than usual while playing, and that he was more in need of a bath than ever. "You're all sweaty," my wife said to the boy when he put up a fight. "No," he snapped, "I sweated when we were at the park. I'm not sweaty now." My wife replied, "You deserved a reward for good behavior when we were at the park. You don't deserve anything but a time-out now." And while the water in the tub turned dirty brown and sandy when our child got in, he didn't really need a bath.

Generic School Supplies Found in Kid's Bag

On Sunday, August 2nd, at the local Target store, I allegedly purchased generic glue sticks and generic scissors for my six-year-old son, instead of the name brands his school insisted my wife and I buy for him by the time first grade started on August 12th. The list of school supplies that officials sent home clearly advised against generic brands. "I didn't buy anything generic," I said on the first day of school when I was brought into the principal's office to explain the generic products found in my boy's backpack. "I do request that someone come forward to give me legal assistance." School officials eventually found the name-brand supplies buried in my boy's bag. Investigators said my son admitted to putting his generic home supplies in his backpack in addition to the name-brand supplies my wife and I bought and packed for him. I was released shortly after my detainment.

Pulling Teeth

MY SEVEN-YEAR-OLD SON'S TEETH WERE LOOSE. ALL he cared about was the money he'd get when the teeth came out.

"Money isn't everything," my wife and I told the kid. I felt his teeth — they weren't coming out any time soon. Thank God! The Tooth Fairy couldn't afford a dollar, let alone two.

The winged tooth-snatcher was off the hook for at least two months.

Three months later, our son's teeth were ready to come out. Three months was more than enough time for the Tooth Fairy to round up some dough.

"What the heck is the Fairy gonna do?" I asked my wife after feeling my son's looser-than-loose teeth.

"How should I know? With all the furlough days the Fairy's getting this year, there's no extra money, not even two bucks."

"Mommy, Daddy," our kid said. There's no way he overheard our conversation. "If the Tooth Fairy can't afford to give me money for my teeth, can *you* give me money?"

My wife and I looked at each other. There was only one answer we could give the kid.

"Don't you worry, you'll get a dollar a tooth just like every other kid in the world."

Our kid leaped for joy, ran to the bathroom and started yanking on his teeth.

"Slow down there, Indie 500," I said, chasing him to the sink. "You don't wanna damage your gums by —"

The kid had already pulled out a tooth.

"But it doesn't hurt," he said.

"But you could ruin your gums forev —"

There went the second tooth.

"That was easy," the kid said. "Look, Mommy," he yelled, running out into the living room with blood pouring from his mouth like a vampire who just preyed upon some helpless victim.

"Mrraaaahhhh!" my wife yelled when she saw the blood. She didn't mind that it went all over the carpet like I was yelling about. She almost made it to the ER with the kid.

"I'm fine, Mommy," our boy said. "I just pulled out my two front teeth."

Meanwhile, I had the Resolve and a carpet brush, trying to get the blood out of our white carpet. "Look what you did," I said. "This'll never come out."

"Carpet isn't everything," our son said.

"No, but money is," I replied. "And we can't afford new carpet right now."

That night our boy called various family members, including Grandpa and Grandma in Northern California, to tell them about his two front teeth.

"Oh boy," Grandpa said over the phone. "Did you know the Tooth Fairy is giving out twenty-dollar bills and video games this year? She might even give you that baseball glove you really want."

Grandpa made sure our boy told us how gracious the Tooth Fairy was going to be that night, all the while laughing at what he thought was a "funny joke."

"Ha ha," I told Grandpa when I got on the phone. "So we'll be expecting the Tooth Fairy from Sacramento tonight?"

"Oh no," he said. "*That* Tooth Fairy passed the torch many years ago."

Our son put his teeth in an envelope and shoved it under his pillow before saying good night.

"Can you believe the Tooth Fairy is giving away all that stuff this year?" our boy said as my wife and I tucked him in. "I hope she gives me a twenty-dollar bill. That'd be the best." He was so excited.

My wife and I said good night to our boy, then trudged into our room to call it a night as well, unsure of what the Tooth Fairy would give our son for his two front teeth.

"It is what it is," I said to my wife.

"But he wants that twenty bucks so bad."

"Money isn't everything," I said.

"It certainly feels like it these days."

The next morning, my wife and I heard our son moving. He was awake. We heard him go under his pillow and rip open the envelope he'd put his teeth in the night before. We waited to hear the disappointment.

There was no response that we could make out. We remained in bed and listened for clues. We heard him moving around the room: rustling paper, scissors at work, tape being pulled from his Scotch tape dispenser on his desk.

Then we heard tapping on our door, which was only slightly ajar.

"Mommy, Daddy," his little voice crept in. He slipped into the room with his hands behind his back. He came to our bed and handed us a folded-up, taped-up piece of paper. My wife and I sat up and opened the paper.

Inside it read, "I love you Mommy and Daddy. This is for all that you do for me." Taped below his writing were the two dollars he'd received from the Tooth Fairy.

My wife and I smiled ear to ear. Our son gave us a smile of his own, a big hole in the front where teeth used to be.

— *May 2011*

Taking Ownership

WHAT AGE ARE YOUR CHILDREN WHEN YOU LET THEM use your computer? How about your iPhone to play games? And the DVR to record programs on TV — when should your kids be allowed to use that?

How old are your kids before you let them use these electronic items unsupervised?

My wife and I have an eight-year-old boy. He's used the computer and our phones many times. But each time we're hovering over his every move; we don't want him accidentally deleting something important or messing everything up.

My stepdad told me that my wife and I are typical only-child parents, that we suffocate our kid, give him no room to grow and mature.

"He has to take ownership of his mistakes," he told me. "It's key to character building."

Later my son asked if he could play a game on my iPhone while I washed the car. My first thoughts: *What if he drops the phone when I'm not looking? What if he deletes something? What if he scrambles up the placement of my apps? Those took me hours to organize.*

I could hear my stepdad's voice from earlier, warning me to give my son responsibility, to let him take ownership if he makes a mistake.

I gave my boy my phone and told him to be careful. And I turned my back.

When I got the phone back, it actually looked OK. My son even asked me if the phone looked like it did when I gave it to him. I told him it did. Wow, maybe this experience was really teaching the kid to be responsible.

"Can I use the computer next?" he asked. My first thoughts: *The iPhone is one thing. The computer has so many things he can screw up when I'm not looking, more important things like system preferences, our checkbook and the order in which I have applications placed on my dock.*

But there was my stepdad's voice again, telling me to let the kid take ownership.

I got the kid set up on the computer and told him to be careful. And I turned my back.

When he was finished an hour or so later, I checked out the machine. What the heck? Nothing was totally destroyed.

So I taught him how to use the DVR, gave him full reign of our electronics in the house. I'm gonna get an award for being the best parent, teaching my kid responsibility so early on.

And then came the problems. My wife found 20 new Words With Friends games started with unknown people on her phone. We got over $30 in receipts from iTunes, showing purchases neither of us had made for applications like "Icee Maker," "Cake Decorator" and some werewolf hunter game that made no sense.

The DVR had no more space available to record. But the memory wasn't taken up by cartoons or other kids shows. It was full of game shows like "Jeopardy," "Wheel of Fortune" and "Family Feud." That's our son.

Then I found the real problem. I checked the computer and discovered missing application icons on the dock. Worse, the icons that were there were in the incorrect order.

My wife and I discussed taking away the kid's electronics privileges. Obviously he couldn't be trusted.

"I'm so sorry I messed everything up," our son said, taking full ownership. "I didn't know I was starting new Words With Friends games with people you don't know. And when I was playing this game on your phone, this ICEE Maker window kept popping up and I just pressed OK to try to get rid of it."

In his defense, some of those free apps do allow tricky pop-up windows that could easily lead to accidental purchases. Even I've almost done that. As for the missing application icons on the computer dock and the rearrangement of the present icons, my wife wrecks that stuff all the time.

When I was a kid, my stepdad taught me how to work on cars. He didn't just show and tell. He told me how to do the work and I did it. While working on a carburetor one time, I actually broke something very costly. I feared for my life.

But my stepdad wasn't upset. The cost to replace the broken part wasn't as valuable as the experience he was giving me, and the ownership he was teaching me to take.

Likewise, my wife and I didn't take our son's electronics privileges away. We pointed out the mistakes he'd made and showed him how to avoid other problems like them in the future. And we told him we weren't upset about his mistakes. We taught him to own up, that not owning up was far worse than making the mistake.

Last week, FedEx showed up at our door with one of those Roomba vacuuming robots. Our son wasn't taking ownership of that one. But my wife and I sure did. It cost us over $200 plus shipping and handling to own that thing.

And that's the story of how our carpets came to be vacuumed automatically on a daily basis.

— August 2011

MORE BITS FROM THE 'BURBS

WINDY OUTSIDE

My son and I took out the kite today to celebrate the wind. We saw someone's car fly away.

LICENSE PLATE BORDER

This lady's plate read, "Loving life as Mommy & Wife." We watched while that life lover had a meltdown trying to yank her bawling angels out of the car.

PARENTING

COMING OF AGE

I ushered my seven-year-old son into manhood this morning. We had breakfast at a counter.

BUSTED

My five-year-old son found a tear in his prized teddy bear. I got hold of some neighborhood kids. Tall girl gave me the dope on a possible suspect, said this kid had a long criminal past, that he'd busted wheels off toy trucks, bit the heads off toy soldiers. Most telling, he'd ripped the wings off a stuffed duck. All I needed was to place this kid anywhere near the crime scene. Then I'd be free and clear. That tear was an accident. Honest.

LIFE LESSONS

My son and I were in the "business meeting area" of a hotel. I told the kid to be serious because this was a serious area. "No being silly. No running. No laughing." Just then, a businessman on his cell erupted into laughter. My son was quick to point out, "He's laughing, Daddy." "He's not laughing, son," I told him. "He's trying to make a sale."

67

The Good, the Babies and the Manly

MY SON WAS ABOUT TO START FOURTH GRADE AND that meant one thing to me: Would I let him go trick-or-treating with just his friends this Halloween?

I went trick-or-treating without parents when I was in fourth grade. But allowing my son to do it? Maybe I'm overly protective. My mom said I was just sentimental, that I liked making memories with my son.

Yeah, you could say that. I wanted to enjoy trick-or-treating with my son before he grew too old for the tradition. I wanted to take him to class on the first day of school before it became embarrassing.

"You're just motherly," said one of my buddies.

"What? Motherly?" I replied. "I'm a man. I'm a carnivore."

"You burn your meat," my friend said. "Men eat their meat raw."

And so began my quest to prove I was a man. The first thing I did was run a Clint Eastwood movie marathon at home. Then I invited some man friends over for poker night.

"Can you watch the language?" my wife asked me. "Our son can hear you."

"He needs to hear me," I said. "That's how men talk."

I invited the kid to the table. He got bored with cards. Clint Eastwood didn't do it for him either.

"I'm gonna see what Mommy's doing," my son said. And he left the room.

"Like mother like son," said one of my friends, snorting with laughter. "Where's the beer?"

I had no beer in the house. I'm not really a beer drinker.

"I drank it all," I said. Then I hollered at the wife. "Wife, go out and get us beer."

My wife ignored me. The night ended shortly thereafter. The guys grew tired of playing poker with fake money and iced tea.

The next day I taught my son how to make his room look like a man lived there.

"This place is too clean, too organized," I said. "You gotta trash it if you wanna be a man."

I cracked a few picture frames, spilled over a bookcase, emptied his pencil jar onto his desk. I ground dirt into the carpet and unmade the bed. Then I wiped the walls with dirty laundry to give the place that locker room smell. I even spit on the floor.

"You know how you hate taking showers?" I said. "Men don't shower more than once a month."

"Mommy's not gonna like this," my son said.

"Men don't worry about what mommies think," I responded. "Let's go trash the rest of the place."

After that, we ate junk food. Lots of it. My son said it tasted unhealthy going into his body. He suggested eating a salad to compensate.

It got *real* bad after that. The kid sat in the spit used to decorate the house and he got so grossed out, he wanted to take a shower. It hadn't even been a whole day yet.

That night, my wife said I'd been taking the man thing too far. She didn't want to talk to me. I couldn't even hang out with my friends. They ditched me to play poker with real money and alcohol.

I went to the store and bought beer — the real dark stuff, man stuff. I watched Clint Eastwood on TV. This was good. This was what real men went through. Real men were loners, like Clint Eastwood's character in those spaghetti westerns. Real men drank beer that tasted real bad. Real men didn't think about anyone else's feelings, not even their own. In other words, I *wasn't* a real man.

So I got rid of that nasty ale, cleaned up the house, apologized to my family for trying to be someone I was not, and I told my kid I'd be taking him to school on his first day.

At school, though, my kid wanted nothing to do with me. He talked to his friends about Clint Eastwood, about not taking showers and his messy room, and about hating school.

When I picked him up six hours later, I dug into him.

"You see this picture on my phone?" I asked. "Is that you in the picture at school today? Is that a smile on your face? Is that what hating school looks like? You don't have to try to be someone you're not."

"I get your point," he said. "But you don't understand what it's like being a man in fourth grade."

My son and I talked about our need to put on a show for others. It was then I knew he still needed me. He still wanted me around. He still loved his daddy.

I smiled.

Then he asked if he could go trick-or-treating with just his friends this Halloween instead of with his mom and me. I guess boys will be men, even my son.

Where's that beer?

— August 2012

Can't Have Trust and Eat It, Too

OUR NINE-YEAR-OLD IS A GOOD KID. HE DOESN'T LIE. He doesn't sneak.

I couldn't trust him at all. Things were going too well. And so came the whole looking-up-poop-on-the-school-computer-and-lying-about-it incident. Our son's teacher sent home a letter detailing the matter. My wife and I asked the kid to come clean, said we wouldn't get mad. We knew how to get the truth.

The kid said he didn't do it.

That lie turned into another lie about his classmate *actually* doing it. And that lie led to our letter to the teacher, which led to our son trashing the letter, which led to our son lying about trashing the letter.

After my wife and I caved, unable to get the truth we knew how to get, the kid confessed.

Then he asked if everything was better.

"No," I said, standing firm as the boss. "It's not better. I can't trust you, and that's not good."

The kid's head fell.

"What if I make a chart?" he suggested.

My son loves visual tools to chart his progress. He recently charted the number of chores he accomplished leading up to the number of chores he needed to earn a video game. We've found that charting works with our kid.

"Charting our trust won't work," I said, still standing firm, still the boss. "You just have to prove that we can trust you."

He tried the head-fall thing again. Pathetic. Like I'd fall for tha —

"Fine," I told him. "You can make a chart."

For each lie the kid had told, my wife and I charged him one week to prove his trustworthiness. We charted out a month. Every day he proved to be trustworthy, we'd check off a box. After the kid had 31 boxes checked off, we'd trust him again. That was the deal.

I wasn't worried about me. I'd make my son earn those days of trustworthiness. I was worried about my wife. She was the pushover — she'd just hand over the days. I had to be the firm one, the boss.

The first day, I told my son he could mark off three boxes for his good behavior at school.

"Three boxes?" my wife exclaimed. "I thought he could earn only one box a day."

"Give the kid a break," I said, standing firm as the boss.

The next day, our son admitted to goofing off in class. He knows better than to goof around like that.

"I'm proud of your honesty," I said, giving him a high five. "Mark off five boxes on the chart."

"Hey, Daddy," my son said. "So really, all I have to do is do bad things and confess, and I can earn back your trust in, like, five days."

I could see what he was doing, trying to get the best of me. I wasn't falling for that.

Before I could fall for that, my wife overheard the conversation and intervened.

"We don't reward bad conduct," she said, "even if you confess. You're supposed to confess."

"Yeah," I agreed, standing firm as the *real* boss. "You still have to be good. From now on, if you're bad and you come clean, we'll mark off only two boxes."

I was getting pretty good at this. My wife was good, too. She wasn't the pushover I thought she was.

The next day, our boy finished his chart. He'd earned our complete trust back.

And then we caught him in a lie — he'd falsified his trust chart, marking off more days than we allowed. Then he lied about doing so. Our kid was treating this like a game, and that stupid chart wasn't helping.

"Can I make a new chart to earn your trust back?" the kid asked.

"No," I said. "I can't trust you, and that's not good. No chart is gonna fix that."

I didn't know what to do. My wife and I talked it over. We decided to trust our instincts. No chart could dictate whether or not we could believe our son. We had to just trust him. And I didn't.

It's now been a month. My wife and I have been on our son like CSI, checking his every move, even when he stirs in his sleep. He's not told one lie. He's not been sneaky. He's even been good in school.

"Have I earned your trust back yet?" my son asked.

I was firm, the boss, and wasn't going to give in like before.

"Heck yeah," I said.

My son smiled. Then he ran off to his room to draw. I smiled. Then I shot over to the secret surveillance video bank in the office closet to see what the kid was *really* up to.

— *May 2013*

CHAPTER THREE

Holidays

The Most Wonderful Messes of the Year

The Son of Halloween

IT WAS A DARK AND STORMY NIGHT.

Well, it wasn't exactly storming outside, but this story works better with wind and pouring rain, lightning and thunder — KABAM! BAM!

"No, don't go up there," my wife warned me. Her forewarning came too late — 32 years too late. I'm a man, after all. I was born stubborn.

"Why are you looking at me like that?" my wife asked as I stared her down. Even my son seemed frightened of me. I cackled like a mad scientist, then I turned, climbed up into the rafters of my garage, and pulled down an old black steamer trunk.

Inside were various knives, axes, torture devices, grisly body parts...and other terror-ific Halloween decorations. I rubbed my hands together with evil glee as I stared at the ghoulish contents, then I noticed my wife and son still watching me.

"What are you looking at, you meddling fools?" I asked in my wickedest voice. "I don't like when people see what they're not supposed to see."

"Mommy, what's happened to Daddy?" my five-year-old son asked nervously. "Is he crazy?"

"Yes," she said. "He's cursed with too much Halloween spirit."

"I told you meddling fools to beat it!" I said.

KABAM! BAM! Lightning and thunder crashed down, scaring them out of the garage.

Once they left, I got to work, turning our home into a haunted house. In the front yard, I strung up spiderwebs all over the trees. I set out gravestones and wooden goblins and monsters that would greet trick-or-treaters on Halloween night. From a stereo system in my garage, I blasted some scary sounds — no, not country music, but chilling sounds of Halloween.

My wife came out and told me I was too loud and would disturb the neighbors.

"Quit meddling," I said in my mad scientist voice. "Nobody will complain, you fool."

Five minutes later, the complaints came rolling in.

"Ah, but listen to the sounds," I told a group of neighbors in my driveway. "Monsters in the night. What sweet music they make."

"He's nuts," one neighbor said. "We're gonna call the police."

"How dare you threaten me," I said, "when you race your loud cars up and down the street in the middle of the night as if there were a checkered flag and a trophy ceremony at the end of the block? How dare you complain about my holiday spirit when your cats use my lawn as a litter box? I have so many dead spots on my grass that I could use my yard as a Twister game mat. You call the cops, and you'll be sorry. You'll all be sorry."

KABAM! BAM! Lightning and thunder crashed down again.

I sent my neighbors away, and I got back to my work.

My neighbors gathered in the cul-de-sac.

"He's not that much of a nuisance," one person said. "He's only putting up his Halloween decorations. Not even the cops could do anything."

"She's right," said the leader of the group. "The cops aren't going to do anything. He isn't doing anything illegal." Everybody agreed, and then the leader said, "Everyone grab some torches. We're gonna burn him out of the neighborhood."

And that's when my neighbors — now an angry mob — surrounded my home with fire.

"You'll never take me alive!" I shouted from the rooftop, while stringing up a ghost on a pulley system from my house to a tree in the front yard.

My neighbors set my house on fire, but even a major blaze couldn't stop me from my greatest Halloween decorating achievement yet. I continued dressing my home and finished my work while under attack, then I ended my pretend evil scientist / angry mob scenario — I became myself again — and I went into the house and asked my wife and son to come outside to see what I'd done.

"But you told us *fools* that you didn't want us *meddling* in your work," she said. "Thanks, but no thanks. We'll stay right here."

KABAM! BAM!

— *October 2008*

Guide to Halloween

MAYBE YOU'RE A YOUTHFUL TRICK-OR-TREATER SEEK-ing insight on how to collect large quantities of candy this Halloween. Maybe you're a concerned mother hoping to ensure that your little Halloween candy hunters are safe. Or maybe you're a justice-seeking father who doesn't want to see his kid lose another costume contest to someone dressed as a toaster oven. Regardless of who you are, this Guide to Halloween will help you enjoy All Hallows Eve to the fullest.

Why am I qualified to write such a guide? As a young trick-or-treater, I always received lots of candy, I remained safe year after year, I won plenty of costume contests and I always had tons of fun. Most importantly, I never got caught.

COSTUMES AND COSTUME CONTESTS

The scariest costumes aren't always the best costumes. The cleverest costumes aren't the best either. Not even the cutest outfit is the guaranteed winner. If you want your child to win a Halloween costume contest, there's really only one thing you can do — get on the judges panel.

FOR TRICK-OR-TREATERS ONLY!

The best way to get lots of candy, let's face it, is to be five years old. For those of us who are slightly older than five, who lack the same cuteness and innocence, here's what you do: First, you need a really adorable Halloween costume. Second, you need a few dozen pillowcases for candy collection. Third, you need a second pair of shoes. Fourth, hit the streets early — before your "eight p.m. bedtime."

At each door, ring the bell and kneel down into your second pair of shoes. When people open the door, they'll find the cutest "little" kid who ever walked the streets, one who deserves handfuls of candy.

To guilt the candy giver into giving you even more candy, find a neighborhood on a hillside where the houses have steep driveways and long sets of stairs to the front doors. (Scout for such neighborhoods several days in advance so you don't waste precious trick-or-treating time looking for the right homes.)

Next, purchase one of those five-foot-tall laundry hampers — the real heavy ones. What for? For carrying the loads of candy you'll surely receive. And don't forget your second pair of shoes.

When candy givers see you, a three-foot-tall angel of joy on their doorstep with a hamper the size of King Kong, they'll feel obligated to give you extra treats because they know you had to haul that giant container up their driveway and up their stairs, and they know you have to lug the thing back down. If you pretend you're out of breath, some candy givers might offer you cash. Score!

If you're lucky, while trick-or-treating you'll come across a haunted house that someone built in the garage. Go in. Haunted houses are great fun, especially when monsters jump out at you and scare you out of your mind.

More thrilling is finding a *real* haunted house. When I was young, my co-trick-or-treaters and I sometimes came across real haunted houses toward the end of the night in unfamiliar neighborhoods. These were the houses your parents warned you about — the ones with guys inside who do bad things to kids. My advice is, beware of houses like these. If you come by one of them, keep your eyes peeled for danger…and when you get to the door and ring the doorbell for "trick or death," be prepared to run really fast. That's what I call real fun.

HALLOWEEN SAFETY

Parents beware: troublemakers are after your kids' candy. If your children collect lots of treats, they'll probably get hassled. To prevent this, you could tell your kids to eat their candy as they collect it, so they'll be empty-handed all night.

Some parents are worried that evil people will tamper with the candy they give out — like putting needles in candy bars. My advice: make candy givers sign release forms (I'm sure you can find these on the Internet) before dropping any goodies into your kids' bags. Maybe have one of your trick-or-treaters go as a lawyer to "administer" the process.

HOSTING HALLOWEEN

Giving out candy seems easy, right? Wrong.

First of all, don't give out non-candy items like crackers, cookies or, the worst, apples. Wax lips just confuse kids. Money isn't a horrible treat, unless you only hand out a few pennies and a nickel. Under no circumstances should you give out pens with your real estate agency printed on the side, or you're asking for kids to use your home as a crash site for airborne jack-o'-lanterns.

If you're not going to be home for Halloween, don't leave a bowl of candy on your doorstep with a note saying, "Take only one piece of candy, please," unless you plan on putting candy out in the flowery crystal bowl your wife has on display in your dining room — the one you've been trying to get rid of since you got the hideous thing on your wedding day.

Aside from that, hand out full-sized candy bars and large bags of name-brand candy, and you'll be fine.

Closing Disclaimer

I'm not one for disclaimers, but my wife reviewed this Guide to Halloween and thought it might be a good idea to offer some helpful words of caution. She warns: "Please disregard the preceding Guide to Halloween, for my husband knows not what he's talking about."

— October 2008

Family News in Brief

Spaghetti for Brains Not Wise

A Halloween carnival volunteer in her early 60s quit mid-shift last Sunday afternoon, following an incident where she asked a teenage guest to stick his hand in a bag she was holding to feel live brains (actually cooked spaghetti). "The spaghetti wasn't so bad," said the carnival guest who wishes to remain anonymous, "but did she really need to put spaghetti sauce on the pasta to sell the whole 'bloody brains' gag?" The carnival volunteer, who also wishes to remain anonymous, said, "Be it as it may, did the kid really need to hurl the spaghetti in my face? I'm a mother, a grandmother, a retired teacher and a community volunteer. That kind of behavior is uncalled for." Both the woman and the teen said they spent the better part of the evening trying to get the garlic and onion smell off their persons.

Boy Seeks Rehabilitation

My five-year-old son checked himself into his room earlier this week for Halloween candy abuse. He admitted to sneaking goodies leftover from Halloween on four occasions within the course of a day. "My son is surprisingly honest with his parents," my wife said yesterday. "And he knows when he's being too silly because of too much sugar. I think he just wants to cut down on the sugar intake, and we're here to support him." After an hour and a half in his room alone, the boy came out clean and with a new outlook on life.

Boy Doesn't Fall for My Santa Claus

At 5:15 p.m. on Wednesday, December 24th, I dressed up as Santa Claus to surprise my five-year-old son during our Christmas Eve festivities with extended family. "The suit looks amazingly real," my wife said before I made my appearance. According to other guests, I made a wonderful jolly old St. Nick. My son agreed when he saw me. "I love your Santa Claus suit, Dad," he said the instant I arrived on scene. "Why are you wearing it?" Even my best acting skills couldn't convince the kid that I was Santa, not Dad. Sources said my boy wasn't tipped off. At 5:22 p.m. that same evening, I dropped the Santa Claus routine. The total loss was $200 for the Santa suit and many good years of my son's belief in the big man wearing red.

Off Without a Thanksgiving Hitch

IT'S THANKSGIVING — TIME FOR MY ALFRED HITCH-cock movie marathon!

My wife and nine-year-old son roll their eyes.

Hey, it's tradition.

I get that they don't get how Hitchcock suspense movies have anything to do with a holiday about giving thanks, about family. On the plus side, however, Thanksgiving is about turkey, and Hitch did cook up one heck-of-a film about birds.

I don't quite recall how watching Hitchcock films on Thanksgiving came to be a tradition of mine. I think there were a couple of Thanksgiving holidays in a row where I happened to be in the mood for a slice of murder, then one year I went without and I knew I was missing something delicious.

The next year, I made sure to watch *The Birds*. The year after that, I watched *The Birds* and a few other Hitch classics. Last year I made plans for the tastiest Thanksgiving Hitch movie marathon of all. I had the entire holiday programmed through dinner, with all the trimmings and *Psycho* for dessert.

I showed my wife a printout of the movie lineup. She actually exhaled into my face, flipping the paper back at me without giving the mix of films any consideration.

Great, I wondered, *what'd I do this time?*

Turns out that she was annoyed with me for making, what she defined as weird plans for Thanksgiving Day.

"*Weird* means it's not normal," I said.

"It's not normal," she replied.

"No, I *normally* watch Hitch movies every Thanksgiving. It's tradition. So it *is* normal."

"It's *not* normal," she said, "to bring movies to someone else's house and play them on their TV during a holiday gathering. We are not playing Hitchcock movies at my aunt's house for Thanksgiving. It's not normal."

That settled it. I'd make it the new norm.

I chopped a few films from the lineup to slim it down for our visit, and packed up my DVDs for the long voyage to my wife's aunt's house. *This,* I thought, *will be the best Thanksgiving yet.*

Days before the gathering, family members discussed what they hoped to do on the holiday. Some planned to watch football. I figured I'd just check scores for them in between movies. My wife and her aunt planned to spend quality family time together. Who does that anymore now that we have iPads? My son planned to go on a turkey-egg hunt. Where do you even find turkey eggs? Maybe that was the point.

First thing Thanksgiving morning, my brother called and asked if I was going to play Duck Hunt. I forgot about that tradition, which died long ago when I retired my old Nintendo video game system. The death of one tradition was all the more reason to keep my Hitchcock movie tradition alive.

On the ride over to the Thanksgiving festivities, I realized my plan was too perfect to work. I couldn't just thrust my movies onto the whole family.

But maybe I could.

Then my wife asked if I left the DVDs at home. I told her I hadn't. She reminded me why I made a mistake — she'd make my life miserable if I asked to play them on her aunt's TV.

Good enough reason.

I brought the movies into the house anyway. Rather, I smuggled them in with the bag of side dishes my wife prepared — just in case I got the opportunity to play them, but I knew I'd have to swallow the excitement I had for a day with Hitch and take part in everyone else's traditions.

By the end of the night, I hadn't even mentioned my movie marathon. In fact, I'd forgotten all about it. I was having such large portions of fun spending time with everyone and hunting down turkey eggs and watching football and eating and not watching any of my films, that I really forgot all about Hitch. *Really*.

On the way home, my wife thanked me for not pushing my film festival on the family.

"It was really a great Thanksgiving," I replied. "I didn't even need my Hitch movie marathon."

After 12 years of marriage, I've learned to compromise. And I feel good about it, like a good husband, a good father, a good person.

But this Thanksgiving is another story.

Now for this year's lineup of Hitchcock films...

—*November 2012*

Shop 'Til You Pop

IT'S THE MOST WONDERFUL TIME OF THE YEAR, OR SO a popular Christmas song tells us.

I love the Christmas season. Come the first of December, a different kind of happiness takes over my soul, an unmatched feeling of joy, of loving, of giving. I know, however, that such isn't the case with everyone.

On Thanksgiving Day, a friend asked if I was ready for Christmas shopping. Nope, not me. The thought of buying presents at this time of year kills any visions of sugarplums dancing in my head. Because people are crazy.

I had no plans for going out into that jungle of shoppers to spend money on items that were marked up just so they could be marked down and advertised as "great deals." To avoid such horrors and pain, I did my shopping in June. Smart thinking, eh?

Then the Christmas season blew into town with the colder weather, and that December happiness came over me, that unmatched feeling of joy, of loving, of giving. I was ready to hit the malls.

Even though I already had gifts for everyone, there were so many other things I could buy. And so many "great deals."

Saturday morning I packed the family into the car and set out for adventure.

At first, I didn't notice the hostility on the road. Motorists cut me off and ran red lights like any other day, but when one lady blew through a stop sign, almost hitting me, and threw her half-eaten candy cane at my car signaling me to get out of her way, I realized, *Today is different—people like this woman have to get to the malls 30 or 40 seconds before me.*

At the parking lot, those 30 seconds paid off for Candy Cane Lady — she got the last parking spot. Just as I was about to park in another country, I found a spot that had just become available — right near the store entrance. Ha! I got into the store 50 seconds faster than Candy Cane Lady… and I got stuck at the edge of three million shoppers in a structure that only accommodated a few hundred.

Children screaming and people pushing made me think this scene wasn't the "meeting smile after smile" feeling that the song "Silver Bells" had in mind.

A wave of perfume crashed into me, making my brain throb. I could feel the side effects — I couldn't think. I pit-stopped my family in a corner of the store near a holiday display and almost got run over by a man carrying several shopping bags. This guy actually sped up, trying to ram me with his holiday treasures, telling me, "I'll run over people like you."

"Like who?" I asked. "Someone not clearing a path for you? Who are *you*?"

Before I could ram *him* with the object in my hands, my wife took our eight-year-old son from my grasp.

A few purchases later and well into the experience of numerous shopping bag handles cutting bloody lines into my hands, I looked up through a skylight in the building and into the heavens, and asked, "Why me?" I wasn't feeling sorry for myself. I was livid. Why me? I finished my shopping in June.

I began making deals with store employees — "If you show me a back way outta this place, I'll give you all my purchases." I even offered up my "next in line" spot at a register to a woman 300 people behind us so she'd turn off her dancing reindeer hat that looped the same "Jingle Bells" tune so often and so loud that it was all I could hear. The sound of the kid crying next to me didn't even register in my ears.

I didn't care anymore. I crashed in the food court. Finally I got a break, but even a super sub sandwich couldn't bring me back to life.

I watched families fight over what they were going to eat. Shoppers threatened other shoppers with plastic eating utensils to win the last table available for dining. People left trays of trash in tree planters because they didn't want to walk a few more steps to the trashcan. I felt disgusted with humanity.

After finishing my lunch, I gave my wife the car keys, got up and got out of there. I walked home and brought up the Internet on my computer to finish the shopping I didn't need to do in the first place — ah, that December happiness was back, that unmatched feeling of joy, of loving, of giving.

Online shopping was uneventful — a few clicks... done, but it was hassle-free.

When my family returned from shopping, they spilled into the house like a party that just arrived, but I knew their laughter and excitement and funny stories weren't real. I knew that going to the malls at this time of year was *not* fun. It was miserable. There was no excitement, not like with online shopping.

No, I didn't miss anything. Right?

— *December 2011*

BITS FROM THE 'BURBS

NO TOUCHING

At the Halloween store, my boy knows not to touch any-thing. "That mask seems cool," he said. "Daddy, can *you* touch it and tell me what it's like?"

GRANDPA'S DEAD

Grandpa found a bargain on Three Musketeers candy — his favorite Halloween treat. So he bought a couple bags for trick-or-treaters and a couple bags for himself. My wife said, "Grandpa's in Heaven." My son said, "When did he die?"

TURKEY DINNER AND A THOUSAND PUMPKIN PIES

We were hosting Thanksgiving dinner. Our guests asked what they could bring. "Don't bring anything," we said. Every single guest apparently understood that to mean: Bring pumpkin pie. So we ended up with a thousand pump-kin pies! Luckily my wife and I had ice cream for the group, because there was only enough pumpkin pie for me.

Our First Christmas

THE TROUBLE BEGAN WHEN MY WIFE AND I TOLD OUR parents that we'd spend Christmas Day alone.

The last few years, we either woke up on Christmas Day in my parents' home in Northern California to spend the holiday there, or we woke up in our own home and traveled to my in-laws' place to open presents there.

When I was a kid, I hated having to go to someone else's house for Christmas Day. I enjoyed seeing my grandparents, aunts and uncles, cousins and family friends, but I wanted to stay home and play with my new toys from Santa.

So this year, my wife and I decided that we wanted to stay in our own home for Christmas Day to open presents. We'd give our four-year-old son a chance to enjoy the holiday here.

OUR RULES

This year, my wife and I want to get up when we happen to wake up — on our own schedule.

This year, we might want to stay in our pajamas all day. I might not even shave. I might not even shower.

This year, I might want to skip breakfast and lunch altogether, and fill up on holiday fudge. I don't care if I have fudge coming out of my ears, out of my pores. I don't care if I get sick to my stomach. That's what Brioschi is for. (Maalox, if you're not Italian.)

This year, my wife and I want to watch the all-day marathon of *A Christmas Story*, that wonderful Christmas film about a kid on a quest to get a BB gun from Santa. That's right. I want to watch the movie over and over, all day long. I don't care how many times I see that kid get the BB gun at the end of the picture. I always worry there's a chance the ending might be different and he won't get what he wants.

This year, I don't want to clean up wrapping-paper shreds from gifts we'd opened. I want to lie in it, bask in it, slumber in it all day long after a victorious bout with our presents.

Our Dilemma

Aside from feeling a little selfish for wanting to have Christmas alone, my wife and I created some problems. I think we hurt our parents' feelings. It's not like we were rejecting our family — we're spending the prior weekend and Christmas Eve with the family. My wife and I just want to start our own traditions for Christmas Day. Is that a bad thing?

So as soon as I phrase that question, "Is that a bad thing," I immediately begin answering it in my head.

Yes, it's a bad thing. I'm the one who's always complaining about not having enough family gatherings. As a kid, my big Italian-American family got together all the time. These days, the cousins, aunts and uncles come together for weddings and funerals only. I want my son to be around his family as much as possible.

Yes, it's a bad thing because Christmas isn't about presents. It's about family, and now my wife and I are selfishly cutting off our families from seeing us on Christmas Day so that we can devour our fudge, our Christmas gifts and the *Christmas Story* TV marathon alone.

Yes, it's a bad thing, because we hurt our parents' feelings. They wanted to see us, and we're denying them access.

OUR SOLUTION

So we called our parents and said we'd be happy to share Christmas Day with them. We told them that after thinking about it, we'd realized we'd made a mistake.

The response: "No, you need to start your own memories, your own traditions. You make your own rules. It's your Christmas. You can have it."

And so it looks like we'll get our own Christmas after all, this year. I fear we may have buttered our bread for the next few years as well.

— December 2007

The Big Christ-miss Wish

WHY CAN'T MY NINE-YEAR-OLD SON ASK FOR SOME-thing simple this Christmas, like a Ferrari or a jet boat?

There are dads like me all over suburbia, I guess. I'm the kind who wants to get his kid the best Christmas gift ever, so when my son came to me and asked for a miracle, I told him no problem.

My wife was watching *Oprah*, when my son and I walked into the room. The guy talking to Oprah on the show said he'd died, seen Heaven and come back to life to tell the story. It was utter ridiculousness.

My son ate it up. And he wanted leftovers — he wanted his grandma to come back to life, too.

"Well," I told him, "that guy was only dead for a few min-utes at best. Grandma's been gone for over a year."

"But that guy went all the way up to Heaven," the kid retorted. "Grandma's in Heaven. So she can just leave and come back down to Earth like he did, right?"

"Well," I began to say, "he — "

"I'll write Santa," my son cut in. "He always comes through." And lucky for me that he does.

The kid got out a piece of canvas card stock (some really nice stuff for a letter) and laid down some of his finest prose. His penmanship was remarkable, something his schoolwork lacked. All the while, my wife and I were trying to convince him to ask for something Santa could actually deliver.

"It's only one thing I'm asking for," the kid said. "Santa won't think I'm greedy."

"But not even Santa can bring a person back to life," I said.

"Daddy," the kid responded with little patience for my petty opinions, "come on. If he can make 300- to 500-pound reindeers fly through the air, and cover 197 million square miles of the Earth's surface in one night in a sleigh, and live forever like he's currently doing, then he should have no problem doing the one simple little thing I'm asking for — bring Grandma back to life."

"Well," I said, "it isn't a…wait, how do you know how much reindeer weigh? And how do you know the square mileage of the Earth's surface? Are those numbers accurate?"

As I steered my phone into Internet mode, my son said, "Go ahead, look it up. But I'm right."

"Well," I said, discovering that he was, in fact, right, "you're not right. And you're wrong about Santa, too. He can't bring Grandma back. I know this because if he could, everyone would ask for loved ones to come back and there'd be all these people coming back to life."

I was sorry to disappoint the kid, but it had to happen sooner or later.

"People *are* coming back to life, Daddy," he said. "Zombies and the guy on Mommy's TV show."

As my son shared his Christmas wish with the whole world, his smile began to turn…into an even bigger smile. No one supported him, but he still believed in the power of his wish until some of his friends told him that Santa doesn't exist. That's what did it.

"Maybe Grandma can't come back after all," he finally said. "With no Santa, there's no hope."

The kid slumped into a chair.

Then, with a renewed energy, "New plan, Daddy!" he said. "We're gonna trap Santa to prove he's real, then we'll just make him bring Grandma back if he wants me to protect his rep at my school!"

"This has gone too far," I said. "I'm gonna have to stop this right now. Son, I have to tell you something — Santa is, well, just too darn big and jolly to trap."

Now, we'd made some killer leprechaun traps and even better Easter Bunny traps over the years, though we never caught our marks. But catch St. Nick? He's a saint. How do you catch a saint?

Using ribbon and garland, a light-up camel from our outdoor manger scene, placebo Christmas gifts, candy cane candles, cookies and milk as bait, and a stuffed snowman to break Santa's fall (it's too complicated to fully explain), we tested the Santa Trap 2900 (patent pending)... on Mommy.

It didn't work. Mommy just got annoyed.

For a dad who likes to get his kid the best Christmas gift of all time, I was succeeding in making it his most disappointing Christmas to date. The trap failure was a real blow to the kid's confidence.

"Maybe *you're* doing something wrong, Daddy," he said. "Or maybe... ah, maybe next year."

"Exactly," I said. "Next year we'll bring Grandma back to life." I'd worry about "the how" later.

"No, Daddy, we can't bring Grandma back to life ever. I think that guy on Mommy's show was just scamming us. We'll just have to visit Grandma at the cemetery for Christmas. How's that?"

And with that, he wrote another letter to Santa, this time asking for a Ferrari and a jet boat instead.

— *December 2012*

MORE FAMILY NEWS IN BRIEF

CHRISTMAS THANK-YOU LETTERS COMING SOON

From the creators of thank-you letters in late July for a wedding that took place almost four months earlier comes a new, heartfelt batch of appreciation on paper to all those who gave Christmas gifts to the Picarella family. Hitting mailboxes across the country this fall, a big thanks from my family will feature profound lines of prose describing what a great time my wife, five-year-old son and I had with our company during the holidays. Recipients can expect our sincere gratitude for the gifts they gave, and even an update on how the gifts have made it into our daily lives. My family and I are truly thankful for a good holiday and also for an excellent year. We look forward to seeing everyone again next Christmas in a few weeks.

MOMMY GETS SPECIAL TREATMENT

My five-year-old son gave Mommy special treatment this Mother's Day. During brunch, when it came time for the kid to use the bathroom, he nominated Mommy to take him. "Since it's your special day, Mommy, you get to bring me," the boy said. When Mommy sat down to watch some TV later in the day, our boy was right there offering up more special treatment. "You can choose whatever show you wanna watch, Mommy," he said. "Do you wanna watch *Teenage Mutant Ninja Turtles* or *Spongebob Square Pants?*" Mommy was reportedly thrilled. Our son also let Mommy give him a bath that night and help him brush his teeth before bed.

"Yay," Mommy said. Before kissing us good night, our boy asked how long until my special day. I told him I didn't get one. Mommy was sure to remind us of Father's Day in June. I can't wait.

Parents Suspect Two Four-Year-Olds to Be an Item

On Valentine's Day, teachers and students reported that my four-year-old son and one of his female classmates were dating. "The two of them were caught together in the tunnel slide sharing a moment of passion," said a teacher, who asked to remain anonymous. "It seems they were sharing a peanut butter and jelly sandwich, something they're both passionate about." Both my four-year-old and the girl denied the alleged romance, stating that they were just good friends. The girl's parents issued a strongly worded statement expressing the lack of seriousness between the couple. "The Picarella boy is very nice, and we'd love to have him over for a play date, but just because we use the word 'date,' doesn't mean that the two kids are dating romantically," the statement read in part. Since these suspicions have come up, my son and the girl have not been seen together again.

We're Getting a New Year!

EVERYONE'S TALKING ABOUT THE BRAND-NEW YEAR that just came out. And most everyone I know lined up for weeks to get it upon arrival on January 1st.

I love getting something new as much as the next person, but getting something new is a big deal to me, and it requires lots of thought and consideration.

Last week, my wife came to me and said she wanted a new year, saying 2008 was full of disappointments and setbacks.

"Can we afford it?" I asked.

"Please," begged my five-year-old son, who'd overheard my wife. "Can we please get a new year?"

I packed my family into the car, and we drove down to our neighborhood shopping center to take a look at the year 2009.

Yes, we stopped by Panda Express to get some fortune cookies.

My wife's fortune told her that a pleasant surprise was in store for her for the New Year, something that could change her life forever.

My son's fortune dared him to dream, hope, believe, seek, feel, find and love in the coming year.

These fortunes were positive signs that 2009 would be a good year.

My fortune, on the other hand, warned me to be extra cautious of new things.

"Why is my fortune the only negative one?" I asked.

"It's not negative," my wife said. "It just tells you to be cautious."

"Yeah, because next year is basically going to be a horrible year for me," I said.

"How can 2009 be any worse than 2008?" my wife asked.

"It can always get worse," I said. "And as a family man, it's my duty to 'kick the tires' on 2009 so we know exactly what we'll be driving off the lot come the turn of the year."

And that's just what I did.

Make and Model

I first took a look at my family's finances to see what kind of 2009 we would be able to get.

It was immediately clear that we'd have to get the stripped-down model. No bells and whistles in 2009 for us.

Maintenance Plan

With a stripped-down model, you've got to know what kind of maintenance plan is going to be required. I took the year 2009 for a test drive around the block to see what was in store for my family.

I foresaw all sorts of problems. I knew then that we'd need some insurance.

Insurance

So where do you go for insurance on a year? I looked to extended family and friends who might be able to offer assistance in the event my family gets stuck on the side of the road in financial hardship.

Basically, there is no insurance for us. I found that most people we know are also getting stripped-down 2009s, and so we'll all most likely break down next to each other.

SPACIOUS?

Going into 2008, I felt I had plenty of room to accomplish some big goals.

This new 2009 model has no room whatsoever. In June, I'll have another birthday, and as I continue to get older, the cap on some of my dreams gets nearer. Pretty soon, these years are gonna start feeling like coach class on most airlines.

WARRANTY

Good fortune or bad, I'm guaranteed that 2009 is going to last my family 365 days ... or our money back. And while it's nice to have a guarantee, I don't know if I really want 2009 to last that long, but I guess none of us have a choice in the matter.

This year certainly looks to be one of the toughest years in recent times for my family. I suppose, if we're cautious, and if we dream, hope, believe, seek, feel, find and love, we may find that a pleasant surprise is in store for us, one that could change our lives forever.

I'm gonna hold Panda Express to that.

—January 2009

Zombies, End of the World, New Year

FIRST THERE WAS THE THREAT OF Y2K, WHERE THE world as we knew it was going to end because all computers, which controlled the planet, weren't going to rollover from '99 to '00. Then there was December 21st, 2012, the last day of the Mayan calendar and thus, doomsday. And finally there was the Zombie Apocalypse on December 22nd, 2012, the doomsayers' way of killing us off if we survived the end.

Well, it's 2013. We made it.

It all came upon us so quickly. When the end is that near, life seems so short. I had put the End of the World in my calendar. I didn't want to miss it. I wasn't sure, though, if I should categorize it as "personal," "home" or "work" since the end of the world really applies to all the above.

I set it as an "all-day" event. My nine-year-old son asked me to skip work that day so he could be with his parents for the End of the World. As luck would have it, I had no more sick leave or vacation days.

On the day, I hoped the End of the World would at least hit before I had to go to work, so I wouldn't have to work another shift. A friend told me the world would most likely end right as I clocked out. That would be my luck.

My son kept his mom and me close that Friday morning of December 21st. It was a somber time, but the end of the world came and went. Life continued.

Next up — the Zombie Apocalypse. And this, unlike the End of the World, wasn't going to be as easy to dodge. That Saturday morning, my son informed me that no one was out front. Apocalypse!

"No one is ever out front," I reminded him. "They're in front of a computer or TV screen."

When I announced that the kid and I had Christmas shopping to finish, he was against going out among the zombies, but assured me with a st-st-stutter that he wasn't af-f-f-fraid. He said it was better if we stayed in. He repeated that he wasn't sc-c-cared. It was just too cold outside, he said.

And then he put on his Davy Crockett hat.

"Alright, Daddy," he gave in, "let's go do some zombie battle."

Zombies were everywhere.

I was wrong: Those people were just mindlessly glued to their iPhones like me.

As the day wore on, however, those mindless people looked more and more mindless. Rather, they were asking for our minds. They chased us, repeating "Brains!" I just assumed we were near Comic-Con.

I'd taught my kid all about Davy Crockett, how he killed a bear when he was only three, how he and his rifle, Ol' Bess, never backed down from a fight. And while the kid had his own Davy Crockett coonskin cap, he didn't have any sort of Ol' Bess to take on brain eaters. The best we could do was…"Run for it!" I yelled.

We took cover at what my son called the World-Famous Diane Camper Christmas Party. For those who haven't yet experienced a Diane Camper Christmas Party, they are, according to my kid, "more world famous than our parties, because more people fit in Diane's house than in ours."

It was the perfect place and time to live life like it was 1999. Diane and her husband, Bones — a doctor, not a magician — offered food, activities, "Star Trek" impersonations and occasional medical attention if injured in a party game. Zombie-bite treatment, however, was questionable, according to Bones.

The place was so packed, my son thought the world was actually all there in Diane's living room. Someone opened the back door to let in some fresh air. They let in some zombies instead. Diane got bit.

"Bones!" I yelled.

"Brains!" he yelled back. He'd become one of Them. And They were everywhere.

The problem with trying to live life to the fullest when you're being pursued by zombies is that it's hard to have fun when you're on the run, ducking tons of clawing, bloody hands and teeth. In hindsight, I suppose we could've had a little more fun with the chase, but when isn't there regret in hindsight?

Oh, there's no place like home for the holidays, and hearing the song with those words reminded my son and me that Mommy was home alone. It's amazing what a boy will do to save his Mommy — my son got us home in one piece, with our brains and all. And Mommy was fine.

When I woke the next morning, I realized, *No, it wasn't a dream. It wasn't a scary story either.*

According to my son's journal, we'd actually lived this crazy adventure. We apparently fought off the zombies using "potty words," a nine-year-old's defense in every tight spot, and now we can finally live every moment like we're at a World-Famous Diane Camper Christmas Party, and enjoy it this time.

Wouldn't you know it? A new end of the world is already upon us. The Big Asteroid deflected off some space junk and is headed our way within the year. This time it's all doom and gloom.

—January 2013

MORE BITS FROM THE 'BURBS

TURKEY TOIL

My six-year-old son traced his hand on a big piece of construction paper and turned it into a picture of a turkey for Thanksgiving. While trying to fit it on the front of the refrigerator, the kid stomped his feet and cried, "I moved the grocery list and I moved Mommy's recipes and I moved my old Halloween pictures — my Thanksgiving art still won't fit." I told him, "Crying won't help you solve the problem." He replied, "I'm in first grade — I don't cry. I whine. So I'm whining."

SANTA'S "RAIN" DEER

My boy told me that the rain comes from Santa Claus. Santa's "rain" deer, he said, fly into the air and, using their magic, make rain so that we'll all keep busy while Santa and his elves at the North Pole make presents for next Christmas.

My son said he didn't learn that from anyone. He taught himself, he said.

HERE AND NOW

Christmas? I'm not even ready for Halloween yet. I only found out yesterday that Thanksgiving's already passed.

Easter Bunny Hunters

MY SEVEN-YEAR-OLD SON LOVES NATURE. HE FOUND a piece of hardened cement and asked me to look at his "shiny new rock."

"This must be sedimentary rock," I said, playing along.

"No," the boy said, strapping on his junior scientist goggles. "It's igneous." He studied the cement more closely. "Daddy, do you think I'm a scientist because of how I discover enchanting stuff in nature?"

"Sure," I said.

Hey, if a piece of cement makes my son that happy, I have to go along.

Now the kid wants to discover everything in nature — weeds, bugs, different shades of dirt. His latest challenge is to catch the Easter Bunny for scientific examination.

"Daddy," he said, "did you ever catch the Easter Bunny when you were a scientist my age?"

"Sure," I said, still going along.

"Don't you think he's out all week hiding eggs and don't you think we can catch him?"

"Sure," I said. Hey, if catching the Easter Bunny makes my son ... wait! What was I saying? Catch the Easter Bunny?

"Actually, son," I backtracked, "the Easter Bunny can't be caught. He'll just disappear."

"Disappear?" he exclaimed.

Then came my big mistake: "My brother and I caught him in a box and we saw him disappear."

"You saw him disappear?"

And so began our scientific adventure. We took out the leprechaun trap we used on St. Patrick's Day (that's another story) and painted over the green with pastel colors for Easter.

"Should we set the box up hot-dog style or apartment style?" my son asked. Evidently hot-dog style is the box laid out horizontally and apartment style is the box standing up vertically. We set it up hot-dog style near some bushes in the front yard. My son added a finishing touch — along the side he wrote: *The Bunny Catcher 101526.*

"101526?" I asked.

"I saw it on a TV at Walmart," he said.

"You remembered the item number for a TV at Walmart?"

"Yeah, in case I ever needed a long number for one of my inventions."

Next, we hid behind a tree and watched the Bunny Catcher 101526 for activity.

"Daddy," my son said, "I'm starting to feel like there's no Easter Bunny. We've been here all this time and where is he?"

We'd been waiting only five minutes.

We went inside the house for an Oreo cookie break. My son seemed defeated.

"Erik at school said the Easter Bunny isn't real."

"Who's Erik?" I asked.

"Remember, he's the one who got his finger smashed in the door when I was in kindergarten?"

"Well there's your answer right there," I said. "Anyone who'd stick his finger into a closing door obviously doesn't know much."

"Yeah, well maybe he knows about the Easter Bunny."

It was time to tell my son the truth.

"OK," I began. "My brother and I never caught the Easter Bunny, and we never saw him disappear."

I continued, "The truth is, he can't be caught or seen, just like the leprechaun can't be caught or seen, but you and I put that gold in the leprechaun trap and when we flipped it over, the gold was gone. Just like on Easter our eggs will be hiding. That's all the proof we need to know leprechauns and the Easter Bunny are real."

My son's smile returned, then he said, "You know, Daddy, Easter isn't just about the Bunny and eggs. It's about Jesus rising up out of the ground on Easter Sunday. His resurrection each year is our hope for an eternal life in God's presence."

"Eternal life in God's presence?" I asked.

"I saw it on a card at Walmart," he said. "Cookie break's over, Daddy."

Then the kid strapped on his junior scientist goggles and grabbed a shovel. Now he wants to discover Christ rising up out of the ground in our backyard on Easter Sunday.

— April 2011

It's Swim-dependence Day!

IF THE SUN'S SHINING, MY FIVE-YEAR-OLD BOY WANTS to swim.

"Why can't we go to the pool?" he sulks when his mom and I tell him it's too cold for swimming.

The wind picks up and 50 degrees suddenly feels like ten degrees, but the sun is shining so the kid pleads, "Look, the sun's out. See how burning and hot that thing looks?"

Yup, our kid loves to swim.

It's the Fourth of July, and the boy asks to spend the entire day at our community pool. My wife and I think it's a fun, convenient, affordable idea.

"We'll avoid all that holiday traffic," I say to my wife.

"We won't have to pay high gas prices to drive anywhere," she adds.

"So can we go?" asks the kid.

"Maybe we can even eat lunch at the pool," I offer. "I can barbecue hamburgers on the grill they have there."

"Maybe we can even eat dinner there," suggests my wife. "Steak or chicken maybe."

"Yeah," the kid says, jumping up and down in excitement. "So can we go?"

"I bet we can even get a view of the fireworks from the pool," I say.

"That'll save us on entry fees anywhere else," my wife says.

"So we can go?" the kid says, still jumping up and down.

"Can we do breakfast there?" asks my wife.

"I don't think you can barbecue eggs or pancakes," I say. "But right after we eat breakfast at home, we can head over."

"Yay!" yells the kid. "We're going to the pool all … day … long!"

"Then again," my wife says, "if he's in the water too long, he'll shrivel up like a prune."

"And," I add, "if he's in the water too late, his lips will turn blue like a ghost."

"Ahhh, man," the kid says with a frown. "So does that mean we can't go?"

"I really don't wanna be in the sun too long," my wife says to me. "I'll burn. Even with sunscreen."

"And I really don't wanna be in the water too long," I say, "I'll get sea sick. Even with Dramamine."

"But I wanna go," the kid says. "Can we please go?"

"If *he's* in the water too long," my wife says, "his eyes will turn red."

"And," I say, "If I'm fetching his sinkable toys at the bottom of the pool too long, *my* eyes will turn red."

"So we're not going to the pool," the kid says. "Just admit it."

"I bet the pool's gonna be really crowded anyway," my wife says. "It's the Fourth of July."

"How about we go to the beach?" I suggest.

"Yeah, the beach," says the kid, jumping up and down again. "I can swim at the beach."

"I bet the beach will be really crowded, too," my wife says. "It's the Fourth of July."

"Yeah, and the beach is messy," I say. "Sand in the car, sand in the house, sand in the bath …"

"And there's the whole getting burnt, getting sea sick, getting red eyes, shriveling up and lips turning blue," says my wife.

"… sand in the bed," I continue, "sand in the ears, sand in the clothes, in the washer, in the dryer."

"But why can't we just go to the pool, Mommy and Daddy?" the kid asks, the frown back on his face. "Look at my skin," he pleads. "See how burning and hot it looks?"

My wife and I finally realize we've done a horrible thing to our son. We built up his hopes and dreams of swimming, and we were about to let him down by telling him we couldn't go.

"OK," I say. "We'll go to the pool."

"Yay!" the kid yells.

We get to the pool and, of all days, it's closed for maintenance.

Our son isn't nuts about swimming in the bathtub all day long.

—July 2009

CHAPTER FOUR

A Family Man's State of Mind

Going Mad Daily

Over Overthinking

I EVEN OVERTHOUGHT THE TITLE OF THIS STORY.

I still think I should call it "Overthinking Over" instead of "Over Overthinking." The title, "Overthinking Over," basically says that my overthinking days are over, but that title looks awkward. My current title, "Over Overthinking," seems to say clear enough that I'm done with overthinking — I'm over it.

However, will readers think it means I'm a double overthinker, an *over* overthinker? I guess I *am* a double overthinker, so it would work, but I want readers to know that by the end of this story, I'll be over overthinking, done with it.

Maybe the dual meaning of the title "Over Overthinking" is a good thing — it's ambiguous, makes you think. In fact, I want readers to get the dual meaning.

Now what if they don't get both meanings? What if they only get one?

I'm running out of space here — I better get to the point. As I stated earlier, by the end of this story, I'll no longer be an overthinker. That's because my neurosis recently went into high gear, and nothing can stay in high gear too long without eventually breaking down.

It all began toward the end of summer. My wife and I came to the conclusion that if I didn't get higher-paying work, we'd never see the year 2013. To say this is an overstatement is an understatement.

Actually, no, it's pretty accurate—I had to make more money. As if on cue, I noticed a better job opportunity where I work, a position that would pay exactly what we needed in order to see the New Year.

I really needed the job. And so I didn't think twice about applying. I couldn't afford overthinking. I couldn't have doubt.

No, the overthinking and doubt came after I made my decision and took action, when it was too late to turn back.

I imagined management laughing at me for applying: "This guy actually thinks he's good enough to apply for this job." I figured they'd disqualify me: "Sorry, only everyone else but you can apply."

I second-guessed my resume and letter of interest— *Why'd I attempt humor in my letter?* I thought. *I should've organized my jobs chronologically, not by skill set. And did I overdo it with the glossy paper?*

A few days went by before I got an interview. My brain was at work the whole time.

They're not even gonna call me in for questioning, I thought. *I better keep looking for other work. But I've submitted hundreds of online applications and heard nothing. I'm no good. Maybe the right opportunity isn't here yet. I'm not looking hard enough. Maybe five hours of sleep at night is too much.*

When I got the interview, I was no less stressed. When I left, however, I felt really good about how I did.

And then I thought about it. I did horribly. *Was I sitting up straight?* I wondered. *I think I mumbled. I know I repeated myself. There were those awkward pauses, but I needed those pauses to think. But I overthought. Since when is thinking such a bad thing? Maybe management wants a faster thinker. Maybe the world will end in December as some people predict, making all of this irrelevant.*

I asked myself why I put myself out there for failure. I guess if I didn't apply, there could be nothing but failure. My brain kept spinning out of control while management made a decision. I wrote a follow-up letter, followed up in person and thought about a few other ways to check in. After a laborious debate in my head, I decided against further follow-up action, then I followed up over the phone.

A week and a half later, the hiring manager called me into his office for my yearly review. I got excellent marks, the best I ever received, and then he told me I didn't get the job.

I sat back in my chair and accepted the decision. I accepted my fate. It's all I could do. So maybe I'd financially destroy my family. Maybe the entire world would end.

Or maybe my family *would* be OK. Maybe the world *wouldn't* end. I couldn't change how I got here — overthinking past moves was a waste.

I told my wife the news.

She asked, "Now what?"

I told her I'd just have to continue working hard, continue looking for work.

And she actually felt at ease. To tell you the truth, I felt at ease, too, but what does that mean — to feel at ease? Does that mean I'm not doing all I can to save my family? Does that mean I'm giving up?

Why did I accept management's decision? Maybe I should've challenged it. Maybe they wanted a rebuttal, to prove that I was the leader they wanted for the job...

I wrote that, by the end of this story, I'd no longer be an overthinker.

I guess my story continues.

— *November 2012*

Dirty Harry: Bug Killer

AS SPRING NEARS, MORE AND MORE FLYING INSECTS begin to occupy the night. Come summertime, they're everywhere.

I hate when bugs get into my home. I must destroy them, as their buzzing and their flybys over and near my family's heads drive us crazy.

When going in and out of my house, my family knows to move quickly. If the front door is open too long, an unwanted pest in flight might enter.

I can't sleep if I know there are flying insects in the house. I'll stay up all night until I destroy them. I've been up as late as four a.m. trying to kill the same two flies during a six-hour period. My wife hates when I stay up late with such determination to kill these buggers. She'd rather have the insects loose in the house, but she married me for better or for worse.

One evening last summer, some TV station ran all of the *Dirty Harry* movies. I stayed up all night and watched them. The next night, when a fly came into my house, I became Dirty Harry: Bug Killer.

Using similar dialogue Clint Eastwood used in the fourth *Dirty Harry* film, *Sudden Impact*, I told the fly, "Go ahead, bug, make my day," as the little buzzer whirled around my living room looking for a place to land. It made my day and landed on a wall. I rolled up one of my wife's magazines and spoke to the fly the way Dirty Harry talks to his suspects.

"This magazine is the most powerful flyswatter in the world. It'll rip your head clean off. So you've gotta ask yourself one question: 'Do I feel lucky?' Well, do ya, punk?"

The fly looked at me with his beady little eyes, wondering if today would be his lucky day. I swung the magazine down. I missed.

The same way Dirty Harry Callahan left messes all over the city of San Francisco as he shot .44-caliber Magnum bullet holes into everything around him while going after a suspect, I left messes all over the house. My messes, however, were magazine ink marks all over the walls and furniture, crooked picture frames on walls where I'd swung at the fly and missed, and chairs on the floor that I'd knocked over while running after the fly.

"Are you using one of my magazines?" my wife asked.

"No," I lied. "It's one of *my* magazines."

She believed me.

The fly finally made a deadly mistake. It led me into the bathroom. I shut the door and locked myself inside with him. *He's going down*, I thought. *If he'll just land, I can get him.*

The fly never landed. He just kept flying. You'd think he'd get tired and land. Not this one. He just kept flying around the bathroom. And with stamina developed by chasing my three-year-old son around my house all day, I kept following that fly around with my wife's magazine, waiting for the perfect chance to swat him.

After about an hour of that, I just swung recklessly and repeatedly at the pest. By this time, my wife was in bed trying to sleep. It was past midnight and I was still up trying to kill the fly.

Boom! Bang! Smash! These were the sounds my wife had to endure as I tried to swat the fly in the bathroom. She came to the door and, somewhat like the way the San Francisco mayor talks to Dirty Harry in the original movie, said to me, "You can swat that fly all you want, but just be in bed by three a.m. That's my policy."

In Dirty Harry fashion, I said, "Well, when a bug comes into our house with the intent to buzz around our heads and drive us mad all night, I stay up for as long as I need to until I destroy the bugger. That's *my* policy."

With fortitude and skill, I zeroed my concentration in on that fly, and then swung my wife's magazine one final time. BOOM! Fly guts splattered all over Britney Spears's latest cover picture.

"I got him!" I yelled. I danced around the fly's corpse, which was lying on my bathroom floor. "That'll teach you to come into my house, hammerhead," I said to the fly as if his spirit, moving on to Fly Heaven, could hear me.

I brought the fly's corpse out to my front porch to show all other flies outside what happens when they enter my house. As I opened the front door to drop off the carcass, three more flies quickly moved in.

Feeling defeated, I recited Clint Eastwood's dialogue from *Magnum Force*.

"A man's got to know his limitations," I said.

I knew my limitations. My son would be running me around the house in two hours. I let those flies live, and I went to bed.

— *February 2007*

Family News in Brief

Telemarketer Scene Offers Ironic "Twist" Ending

During one of the worst telemarketing call streaks of our time, Americans are standing up for their rights, demanding that telemarketers respect dinner as a time to hold off on sales calls. "Before sitting down for that final meal of the day, I take the phone off the hook," said my next-door neighbor, who claims telemarketers are a pain.

Last week, a telemarketer called me while I was eating dinner to tell me I won $25,000. Aware of the oncoming sales hook, I asked the telemarketer to hold while I ran downstairs so I could verbally notify my wife of the alleged reward. With great enthusiasm, I bolted down the hallway and staged a nasty spill, which I enhanced with pots and pans hitting the floor. I acted as if I was in extreme agony, yelling out, "I can see the bone," to which the telemarketer asked in a panicked state if I was OK.

After hanging up the phone, I broke into the obligatory laugh and, in an ironic twist of fate, actually tripped over one of the pans I'd thrown to the ground and, according to medical professionals, twisted and sprained my wrist, making the use of a fork and knife at dinnertime a worse pain than a telemarketer's phone call.

NEIGHBOR CAT RUINS FRONT LAWN

Despite efforts to keep the neighbor's cats off the lawn, at least one feline left a mark that has killed the grass. "I remember a time when my lawn was perfectly green all around," I said in a statement. "Now there's a big ugly yellow spot right in the middle." The said neighbor denies charges against him for aiding and abetting the criminal cat, claiming that his precious pets are all indoor animals. Various sources, however, said they saw the neighbor's black cat cross their path on the sidewalk earlier this month. The damages to my lawn were $13.39 for Scotts LawnPro Step Four lawn fertilizer from the Do-It Center.

Nobody Gets to Drive This but Me

I DON'T LIKE HOUSE CHORES AT ALL, BUT MY WIFE AND I recently bought a new vacuum, and I've since changed my attitude about carpet-cleaning duties.

Let me break down the model we bought. First of all, it's not your typical vacuum. This piece of high-powered machinery has D2. What's D2? D2 is Dual Cyclonic Technology. I still don't really know what that means, except that it gives my new vacuum serious power.

This thing's got something like a 300-amp motor. When it starts up, it sounds like a jet engine. It also has things like a Power Brush, Antimicrobial Technology and something on the back of the machine toward the bottom that says Power. That's what I'm talking about. Power! Oh, that's the "power" switch.

This vacuum is tough. It's got a Scuff Guard on the front of the machine for ramming, it's got wheels that you can take through any off-road course and it has extension hoses that could probably withstand several buckshots.

My new vacuum has a shiny metallic red coat of paint that would put any restored classic car to shame. I've already put a coat of wax on the machine, and it's so shiny and reflective that I can use it as a mirror when I shave.

My old vacuum would miss small fuzzes, pieces of thread and dirt that got ground into the carpet, which is the main reason we replaced the thing — may it rest in pieces. I'd go over the same mess numerous times with the old vacuum, and still it wouldn't pick the stuff up.

Now, let me break down my new vacuum's performance. I have to strap myself into this vacuum before operating the thing. Yeah, it's got *that* much power. Once I'm strapped in, I still have to hang on.

I could pour honey and molasses on my carpet, and this vacuum would pick it all up. I've accidentally sucked up a few of my son's Tonka toys and even grabbed pieces of furniture the way the Death Star's tractor beam grabbed the Millennium Falcon in the movie *Star Wars*. I'm sometimes surprised that my new vacuum doesn't pull the carpet up into the vacuum waste container.

Yes, I actually enjoy vacuuming these days. I invite friends over to the house to show the thing off like it was a new motorcycle. Most of them are envious of my new machine and want to take it for a spin, but a man never lets another being drive his vehicles — vacuums included.

There are the few friends who want to challenge me with their pieces of vacuuming equipment. Of course, they're all talk. Not one of them has shown up for a challenge. Two of them converted to the type of machine I just purchased.

My wife is more than happy that I've claimed the vacuuming duties in the house. Ever since, she's been on the computer surfing the Internet obsessively. After a while, I got a little curious as to what she was doing. I could've just asked what she was trying to find, but instead I decided to play Sherlock Holmes and do a little snooping around.

I went online and checked her search history. I found several Google searches for things like "high-powered glass cleaner," "high-powered iron," "high-powered Swiffer," "high-powered paint brush" and…you get the idea. And I get the idea, too. Maybe this new high-powered vacuum wasn't such a hot idea.

—January 2008

I Don't Wanna Hold Your Baby

YOUR BABY MIGHT BE REAL CUTE, BUT I DON'T WANNA hold it. It's not personal.

When I got a new car, I didn't ask people if they wanted to drive it. When I got my wife, I didn't ask people if they wanted to date her. The car and the wife are mine. And your car and your wife are yours.

If a friend asked me to drive his new car, I'd say, "No. What if I crash and destroy the thing? Worse, what if I fall in love with it?"

If a friend asked me to date his wife — well, I'd say he was an idiot.

Getting back to where I began — I don't want to hold anyone's newborn baby.

"It's OK," the mother always says. "You won't drop her."

"But I just don't wanna hold her," I say. "Why do you *want* me to hold her?"

Why *do* they want us to hold their kids? Are they tired of holding the little guys? Maybe they want a break? If I'm going to get any joy out of holding a kid, it's going to be my own.

"But don't you just wanna love them?" my wife asked when I told her I didn't want to hold her friend's new twins. "They're so cute."

"No, I don't just wanna love them," I said. "If you saw some stranger you thought was cute, would you just walk up to him and cuddle him? I don't know those babies. I don't even know the parents all that well."

Just before my son was born, a family friend asked if I wanted to hold her newborn baby — for practice.

"No thanks," I said.

"But don't you wanna know what it's like to hold your baby?"

"Yeah, I do," I said. "But that's not my baby, that's yours."

"Here," she insisted, "take him." And she forced her baby into my arms.

Before she could let go, I put my hands behind my back.

"I'm not gonna take it," I said. "Please don't make me."

"But you won't drop him," she said.

"If you try to give me that thing, I'm gonna drop it. So don't give it to me."

"But you won't drop him, I promise."

"No," I said, "I'm telling you, I will drop it if you give it to me, I promise. I'll do it on purpose."

For some odd reason, she decided not to be my friend anymore. And when my son was born, she wouldn't hold him — even at my wife's request, which was fine with me. My wife, on the other hand, was worried.

"Why doesn't she wanna hold him?"

"Why do you want her to hold him?" I asked. "What if she drops him? Worse, what if she wants to keep him?"

About two years later, the same lady had another kid. She was so thrilled about it that she even approached me with a friendly smile and asked if I wanted to hold her.

"You wanna feel what a baby girl feels like in your arms?"

I took the baby into my arms. I knew I wouldn't drop her — holding my son so many times had given me the confidence. That's when it happened. I fell in love with the little darling and I wanted to keep her.

So my wife and I tried to have another kid, only we found we were unable to do so. Maybe it was karma after I'd refused to hold so many babies for so long. Or maybe it was meant to be, because now I wouldn't have to share the love I have for my son. Maybe it was just basic physiology.

Today, I have no real problem holding other people's babies, though I don't ask to do so. I also have no problem with the reverse. For example: the other day, I had no problem asking the neighbor if he wanted to hold my groceries. I asked him to hold them from the trunk of my car to the house.

"Your food might look real good," he said, "but I don't wanna hold it."

— *October 2009*

BITS FROM THE 'BURBS

ACTION! SUSPENSE! THRILLS!

Do you want the whole story with all the bloody details, all the heart-wrenching excitement, the twist and the turns? Or do you want the truth?

PUPPY DOG EYES

My dog looks so sad when I leave. His chin drops to the ground. He puts on a frown. His eyes droop. He must know I have to go to work. How else, does he think, would I be able to get him his dog food?

TO SEE OR NOT TO SEE?

I have vision. And I know what a vision board is. I *have* a vision board. It's in the garage somewhere.

LUNCH DOWNTOWN

The place was packed. We all ate alone.

EUREKA, I FOUND IT

My dog isn't looking for anything. He's just sniffing, collecting smells. He's a connoisseur of common "scents."

MASS GENOCIDE

It's sickening. Every day, countless lives are mindlessly taken. I counted 50 pulverized bugs on *my* windshield alone.

All Was Well...and Then...

I WOKE UP YESTERDAY MORNING FEELING GREAT. ALL was well.

I sauntered into the kitchen, flipped on the light. The light worked.

I poured myself a big bowl of my favorite cereal. I went to the refrigerator. We had milk.

My cereal was very good. I didn't rush it. I enjoyed it.

I got cleaned up and dressed for work. I finished getting ready right on time. I drove to the office. I made it there right on time.

When I sat down at my desk, I got to my tasks. I finished everything I set out to do...right on time.

At lunchtime, I wrapped my teeth around some food. It was very good food. I had just the right amount to eat— not too much, not too little. When it was time to go back to work, I was willing and able, and I finished everything I set out to do.

My wife called me at work. She said everything was well. She just wanted me to know that. I told her all was well with me, too. She told me all was also well with our six-year-old son.

After work, I drove home. I made it.

That's when I realized traffic didn't stop me. There were no Sig-Alerts. No construction. The motorist on his cell phone wolfing down an animal style double-double from In-N-Out Burger while grooming his dog and piloting his car didn't smash into me as I drove through that green light.

When I got home, my wife was watching TV. It wasn't a reality show. It was good TV.

The mail in my mailbox was addressed to my wife and me — not to my neighbors or to the people who lived in my house 20 years ago.

I decided to trim some trees on my property. Raccoons the size of small rhinoceroses had been using the trees as their gateway to my rooftop for tap-dance parties that took place in the middle of the night. I dug out my rickety extension ladder, threw it up against the trees and hacked the branches away from the house. My ladder didn't collapse.

When I changed the oil in my car, the cheap-o jack stands I have didn't snap and send the underside of the vehicle into my face for a kiss.

The shower rained warm water on me when I went to clean up for dinner.

My wife had my favorite dinner hot and ready for me when I finished cleaning up.

My son spilled peas off his plate, and the vacuum with an overstuffed pick-up bag still sucked up the mess when I ran it over the floor.

All was certainly well.

And then it kept going well.

"What kind of Friday the 13th is this?" I asked my wife.

I tried to make unfortunate things happen to me, but everything turned out well. I tripped over obstacles I placed in the middle of the floor for the very purpose of injuring myself. I couldn't get hurt.

I tried to start an argument with my wife. She gave me a kiss.

I told my kid he could do whatever he wanted to do and that no matter what he did, he wouldn't get busted. He made an "I love you, Daddy" card.

For a columnist who uses daily events as source material, "all is well" is not so well at all. Stories without conflict are not stories. I have nothing to write about this week, as you can tell if you made it this far. In fact, the following gap is brought to you by that lack of something to write about:

"For some people," my wife said, "Friday the 13th actually brings good luck."

Wouldn't you know? That's just my luck.

— November 2009

I Forgot What I Was Worrying About

I WAS WORRYING ABOUT SOMETHING REALLY IMPORT-ant, but I forgot what it was.

Sometimes I worry about Item A as if it's the end of the world, until Item B comes up, then I forget about Item A, and Item B becomes the new end of the world — as if Item A wasn't anything to worry about in the first place. Once I resolve Item B, I go back to worrying about Item A, and Item A becomes the end of the world again.

That's not the case here. The case here is: I simply forgot what I was worrying about. Now I'm worrying about what I forgot because what if it was important?

I'm retracing my steps, hoping a little déjà vu will help me remember what I was worrying about. I bump into my six-year-old son. I ask if I forgot to do anything for him. He says I'm supposed to make dinner.

"I can't do that right now," I reply. "I'm busy worrying about trying to remember what I was worrying about."

My wife returns from a late-night meeting and I feel relieved — she usually helps me remember what I forget. I ask her, "Did you ask me to do something? I can't remember."

She's crying. She says something about "worst day of her professional life."

"No, that's not it," I tell her.

Before I can get back to retracing my steps, my wife attacks me.

"I just told you I had a terrible day," she says, "and all you care about is what you forgot? How about you forgot to think about your wife?"

My wife and I have an understanding that if we get into a tiff, we have to resolve the issue right then and right there — we can't walk away and let it boil, so I drop everything and tell her we'll argue soon.

Now back to retracing my steps.

"You broke our rule," my wife says, following me around the house.

The problem: When I can't remember something, I go mad and I do things that are out of character. I go even madder if I'm digging deep for something and I can't pull anything up, but somehow I'm sane enough to realize I'm being insensitive. I apologize to my wife and kid and tell my wife I'm ready to hear what happened at work.

I'm not catching a single word of her story. The more she talks, the more it bugs me that I can't remember what I was worrying about.

Maybe I was worrying about writing thank-you letters for Christmas gifts I received. No, I have another six months before that's a problem.

Maybe I was worrying about calling someone or meeting someone or paying someone. I go through my address book, looking for names, hoping that'll refresh my memory. Who the heck is Benji Biffer? Why's his contact information in my address book? Geez, my grandparents are still in my book? They passed away over five years ago.

"Dad, I'm so hungry," my kid says.

"Mike, you're ignoring us," my wife says.

I try to tune out my family and think: *I got home, put my bag here, was gonna turn on my computer, went to the bathroom instead, was thinking about the thing I was worrying about when I went to the bathroom. What if I flush the toilet? Maybe the sound will trigger the thoughts I had when I previously flushed.*

Fffff-shhhhhh.

Nothing.

I had no engagements, no late bills, nothing to do for work. Did I miss a doctor's appointment?

My kid: "Dad, we need dinner."

My wife: "Daddy's not making dinner."

My thoughts: Maybe I was supposed to make dinner.

"Daaaaad!"

"Miiiike!"

"Ahhhh!" I scream. "Will you people leave me alone?"

My wife and kid freeze out of fear.

I finally remember what I forgot! I wanted to get the mail. I noticed my wife brought it in.

—January 2010

MORE FAMILY NEWS IN BRIEF

THE BED SHEETS MUST BE PERFECT

My wife announced yesterday that I'm obsessed with bed sheets and that I need my bed sheets to be symmetrical at all times. If a bed isn't made neatly with hospital corners, she added, then I must strip it down to the mattress and remake it. "My husband has no problem remaking the bed no matter what time it is," she stated, "even with me in the bed." I said, "If my wife wouldn't roll over and drag the sheets with her, I wouldn't have to remake the bed in the middle of the night." My wife asked how she could possibly know what's going on with the sheets when she's asleep. I answered, "I'm always aware of how the sheets are covering my body, if they're straight and proportioned, even in the deepest sleep. You just know." And my wife says *I* have the problem.

Bracelet Clasps Poorly Designed

Jewelry makers still haven't produced a stable bracelet clasp that's easy to hook together. According to sources, the toggle bar clasps come apart too easily. Consumers say the magnetic clasp is a good idea, but it too doesn't hold. The traditional clasps on bracelets, experts suggest, are still the best jewelry fasteners. I disfigure my jewelry before ever coming close to hooking it together. "We can track our friends' precise locations via cell phone technology, but we can't invent a bracelet clasp that's easy to put on and stays together," I said in a statement yesterday. "Since I got a medical ID bracelet (which indicates my heart condition), I must allow an extra two hours each morning to wrestle with the clasp. I suppose I could tattoo my heart condition on my forehead."

Motorized Toothbrush
Terrorizes Household

A motorized toothbrush has been tossed in the trash after going on an unstoppable rampage inside my six-year-old son's bathroom. At about seven p.m. on Tuesday, the SpongeBob SquarePants toothbrush, two months old, was turned on for the nightly cleaning of my son's teeth. That's when it started, and didn't stop until I pulled out the batteries. "What the heck is wrong with this piece of junk?" I said when I learned that pressing the OFF switch on the device wouldn't shut it down. "Turn off, you piece of junk!" My wife captured the incident on video. The toothbrush can be seen just going and going and not shutting off, even when I tried smashing it against the bathroom counter. The toothbrush is currently imprisoned in the trashcan near the side of my house. It faces total destruction on Monday when the trash man comes to empty our bins.

Have Your Cake and Wear It, Too

I LOVE CAKE. SO WHEN I SAW THE TABLE AD FOR chocolate cake at the restaurant, I knew I had to have a piece. My wife was against it. She didn't want our seven-year-old son getting any ideas.

"If you get *it*," she said, "then he'll want *it*, too."

"Want what?" our son asked. "What's *it*?"

"*It*'s nothing," my wife replied, doing her best not to give the kid any ideas.

"*It*'s just cake," I said.

"Cake?" the boy said with increasing excitement. "I love cake. What cake? Chocolate cake?"

"The sugar's gonna make him hyper," my wife warned me.

When the warning didn't make me budge, she reminded me of the messes our kid made with cake in the past. My wife knows I hate messes.

"I can handle it," I said. "It's all under control."

The waiter came by and, on cue, asked if we wanted dessert. My wife said *no*. I told her it was too late, that I'd already ordered.

Then I actually ordered.

Bystanders could see the storm clouds on the horizon when I asked for chocolate cake all around, even for the seven-year-old. They shot up out of their seats and ran, leaving full plates of food.

Out came the biggest…triple-decker…double fudge…towers of chocolate cake I'd ever seen. They came with shovels.

My wife's piece intimidated her. She didn't touch it. I studied my slice, looking for an approach route. My son jumped right in, no plan at all.

The face on the busboy was telling: *Help!* He could foresee cake everywhere. He eyed the kid, looking for compassion. He got no such response. He eyed the mom. The mom cried. He eyed the dad. I gave him a look of pure confidence. I think the poor guy ran for the time clock.

I slowed my eating during my approach into quadrant two of the cake. That's when I noticed the mess my son was making. I got scared. Real scared. I caught the busboy in his travels (he must've been denied clocking out), and I requested a few hundred napkins. He obliged.

I didn't know where to begin. The mess started on the table surrounding the kid's plate, then it spread to the hands. The hands touched the face and the hands touched the shirt and the pants. From there, the mess made its way to the seat, then to the floor. It somehow managed to make its way to the ceiling, too.

Nobody at our table could move — we were marooned, afraid of the mess as if it were a monster or life-threatening bacteria. In hindsight, it wasn't as bad as it seemed.

It was worse.

I left my cake unfinished, and devised various strategies to get the kid out of the restaurant without tracking cake all over the place, and more importantly, without getting cake on me, but I couldn't perfect anything. Making matters worse, the restaurant was pressuring us to leave to accommodate a line of people waiting for a table.

"You have to go," the waiter said.

The busboy grinned, happy to see me in peril — misery loves company. I couldn't pull myself together. Nothing was under my control. The mess was my fault and I had no exit strategy, then a plan came to me: apologize to my wife for being dead wrong about the cake (maybe the first true apology in the history of husbands and wives) and apologize to the busboy for the mess.

The busboy took pity on me. He armed me with a stack of towels and offered me good luck. I welcomed his warmth with gratitude. Then I buckled down for the job I had to do. I wrapped my kid in towels and sprinted out the door.

The towels didn't stop the mess from spreading. I got cake all over my hands and arms, all over my clothes. I made a chocolate cake path out of the restaurant and into the parking lot. The inside of my car was covered in double fudge. It looked like cake had exploded in the back seat, and it might as well have.

When we got home, the mess continued onto the driveway and into the garage. It landed in the entryway, the hallway and in the bathroom. Even the dog, who was in his doghouse out back, found morsels of cake to eat.

My wife and I eventually got everything cleaned up and had our boy ready for bed at 11:00 p.m. — two hours past his bedtime. The kid was so hyped up from cake, he couldn't sleep for another three hours.

Last night, we went to dinner — the first outing in some time. After eating, the waiter asked if we wanted cake. The cakes he showed us on a display plate looked so good. Yum.

"How about a cookie?" I said.

—January 2011

The Dentist
Or:
How I Tricked a Dental Professional Into Thinking My Teeth Were Perfect

SIX MONTHS AGO, MY DENTIST SAID I HAD A CAVITY that needed drilling. He warned me to change my brushing habits immediately or else.

My first thought: *My brushing habits have kept me cavity-free for 20 years. What's he talking about?*

My second thought: *We're in tough financial times—I have no cavity. This guy just needs money.*

I told the dentist I was going to get a second opinion. I left his office and went online.

According to the Internet, I didn't have a cavity at all. Various sites and forums let me know that brushing my teeth twice a day with tartar control anti-cavity toothpaste would help prevent cavities. Well, I brushed my teeth twice a day with tartar control anti-cavity toothpaste. I couldn't have a cavity.

I called my dentist and told him he made a mistake, that my teeth were fine and that I didn't need any filling. He told me I not only needed a filling, but that my gums were receding. Don't you love how he just tacks that on after the fact?

By the way, not only do you need that True Coat Super Seal on your car so you don't get oxidation, but you're also going to need our Shine-E-Gloss on top of that to protect the True Coat.

This guy was a car salesman. What the heck does *receding gums* even mean?

I went to the professionals to find out — I went online. Have you seen what receding gums look like? Yikes! Receding gums cause uncontrolled growth of plaque and tartar, which causes cavities and, later, inflammation of the gums — gingivitis. Gingivitis, I read, is a sign of even worse things to come.

Let me paint the picture: swollen gums (my gums seemed to be swelling the more I looked at them), discolored teeth (mine weren't all that white), bone loss (maybe that tiny piece of bone I swallowed with my steak wasn't from the steak), abscesses (I wasn't sure what that was, but I knew I had it anyway) and bad breath (I needed breath mints all the time).

I called my dentist back, made an appointment to get my cavity removed, then I bought three kinds of toothpaste — one for the morning, one for the afternoon and one for the evening. I also bought a range of mouthwashes, two types of dental floss and a motorized toothbrush that cost 80 bucks.

Next, I amped up my brushing habits. After eating, I'd rinse with mouthwash, floss my teeth, brush my teeth for no less than ten minutes, floss again, and then rinse with a different mouthwash. I altered my diet as well — no fruit snacks or hard candies, very little sugar at all and plenty of dentist-approved chewing gum. Chewing gum after meals, I read, stimulates the production of saliva, which helps wash away and neutralize the acid produced by bacteria in plaque.

Within a week, my teeth felt great. My wife and eight-year-old son even upgraded their teeth-cleaning programs.

They started using my supplies, so I had to start hiding my stuff. I told them to get their own.

One day I couldn't find one of my tubes of toothpaste. I thought I hid it too well. Later I thought my wife or kid used it up.

But how could they go through a whole tube in a few days? I thought.

Then my father-in-law stayed over and used the shower in our guest bathroom. He came out smelling like my son's watermelon-scented three-in-one body wash/shampoo/conditioner.

"What happened to the liquid Dove?" he asked. "All I could find was that watermelon stuff."

My son got defensive. "Girls want their men to smell like fruit. How do you think I got Tess to be my future wife?"

I'm not sidetracking here with the shampoo story. This "shampoo incident" brought me to the empty tubes of my toothpaste in the trash. You see, my son is an amateur scientist — he empties bottles of shampoo, tubes of face wash and now the guest bathroom liquid soap and my super-duper toothpaste into empty water bottles to make "potions." When I found the empty liquid Dove bottle in the trash, I also found my tube of toothpaste — emptied.

It got worse. When I went to get my cavity drilled and filled the following day, the dentist said my teeth looked worse than before and that I really needed to change my brushing habits. What the heck?

I came to the conclusion that my dentist would never be happy. He was a perfectionist and my teeth would never be perfect, not if I was going to use them, so I went back to my old, not-so-great brushing and eating routines. Six months later when I had another checkup, I didn't even do the whole brush-really-good-for-the-dentist-appointment-like-I-brush-this-way-all-year-long routine like I normally do. I didn't care what the guy had to say about my teeth.

"Wow," he said. "Your teeth look great! Didn't I say you just needed to change your habits?"

— May 2012

MORE BITS FROM THE 'BURBS

DO-OVERS

There are times in life when you flub and there's no going back. You can't undo mistakes. I just screwed up — I shook hands with the plumber.

MISERY GETS NO COMPANY

Happy people aren't real, just carefully cast in your life to remind you of how much you haven't accomplished yet.

MANNERS, PLEASE

After returning home from the store, my six-year-old son asked if he had good manners. I still can't figure out what he wants.

BATTERY-CHANGING PILLS WANTED

Calling all inventors, doctors and chemists! I'm the proud owner of a Medtronic pacemaker, which I had installed in my chest two years ago to keep my heart from stopping. In about eight years, I'll need to undergo another horrific surgery so doctors can replace the battery in my device. I will pay good money to anyone who creates a pill somewhat like aspirin, which, when swallowed, finds the pain in a person's body and kills it. The pill I'm looking for will, once swallowed, find the old battery in my pacemaker and replace it with a new one. Those up for the task have about eight years to respond with results. Please send bids to Michael Picarella at michael.picarella@gmail.com.

Milk Mania!

IT'S NIGHT. GOOD GUY IS FAST ASLEEP IN BED, unshakable.

Outside, Bad Guy is armed, dangerous. He breaks into Good Guy's house. If only Good Guy could hear Bad Guy down the hall, he could reach into his end table for that pistol and defend himself.

But Bad Guy enters Good Guy's bedroom. He raises his weapon, aims it at Good Guy…

Just then, Good Guy springs out of bed, retrieves the pistol from his end table, turns to Bad Guy, aims his weapon and pulls the trigger before Bad Guy can even think about firing.

Good Guy has no bullets! No bullets! Bad Guy blasts Good Guy down.

I'm Good Guy in that scenario, and that's exactly what happened to me the other night. Sort of.

I got home very late from work and was hungry. I poured myself some cereal, opened the refrigerator…we had no milk! No milk! It was like being shot in the chest. I couldn't breathe. It was worse than death.

So I woke my wife.

"Sweetie," I said. "Do you know what happened to the milk?"

"We drank the last of it at dinner," she admitted, ratting out herself and our eight-year-old son.

"I wonder if any stores are still open," I said, knowing everything around was closed.

My wife said I didn't *need* my nightly milk. Then she assaulted me with a list of other foods and drinks I could consume instead. I could make a salad or a sandwich, and I could drink some water or unsweetened iced tea. I was wise to her parlor tricks. She always wants me to eat and drink healthy.

"You can make oatmeal," she suggested.

That was an insult. Who likes oatmeal?

I considered a long drive to the nearest open-all-night store I could find, but it was late and my family and I had to get up early in the morning to drive down south for some event my wife planned.

I decided to go without my precious milk that night. I'd just get up even earlier in the morning and run to the store so I wouldn't miss out on my morning cereal and glass of milk.

That's just what I did. I got up *real* early and, as I was making my way out the door, my wife stopped me and asked if I could take our son.

"That'll slow me down," I said.

At the store, my son slowed me down. We had to stop and talk with the librarian from school.

"No more talking to anyone," I said when we finally broke away.

"But I never saw Mrs. H. outside of school," he said. "Now I know what she's like when she's shopping."

I grabbed a carton of milk, but at the register, my wife called me on my cell phone and asked me to pick up a few other items. I left the register, ran through the store to get the stuff she needed and was back in time to wait in a long line during the big morning rush I'd previously missed.

Finally, we got to the car. When my son and I were almost home, my wife called again with one last request. I had to go back to the store. My cereal and that glass of milk could wait.

My son and I eventually made it home and I tore into the grocery bags. The milk was gone.

"Maybe you left it at the store," my wife offered.

"I don't have time to go back and get it," I said. "We have to leave in 15 minutes, and I still have to eat something, shave, shower and pack the car."

My wife and kid sat down for their oatmeal. I made myself some oatmeal, too. I sat and ate it and didn't say a word, but my family sure squawked. Their *yums* and *mmmms* sounded like they were eating the greatest meal ever prepared, and there I was eating what I thought tasted like unflavored paste.

I pushed my oatmeal aside. Got up. Grabbed a water pitcher. Left the house.

I went next door and asked the neighbor for some milk. He said he bought too much, that it would go bad before he could drink it. He was going to call me to see if I wanted it.

Now, when has anyone ever asked if you wanted an extra gallon of milk? That just doesn't happen in real life. But it happened to me. And my cereal and glass of milk that morning were amazing. I even got the family out of the house on time, thanks to my daily serving of milk.

A few days later, as I was driving, I had a thought. I pulled over, opened the trunk, dug to the back, and there it was: the cause of that rotten smell I detected during the drive — the carton of milk I thought I left at the store.

I drank it anyway.

—June 2012

Coffee Head

I HAD NOTHING TO WORRY ABOUT. THE CAFFEINE IN the coffee I drank before bedtime wouldn't keep me awake. I'd get to sleep in good time and be well rested before a very busy day of work.

As I loaded that single-serving K-Cup canister into the coffee machine, my wife insisted the caffeine would not only keep *me* awake, but that I'd keep *her* awake. She had work the next day, too.

"You have nothing to worry about," I assured her. "If I can't sleep, I'll give you one of my famous head rubs."

For your information, I'm going to patent my head rubs. It's not your everyday method. It's the world's only head rub that offers subtle, yet complete relaxation for a tired, yet stressed-out wife of mine in an era of overproduced head rubs.

That's my pitch for the patent board. Too wordy?

My wife knows my process is one of a kind. That's why she gave me the OK and turned in.

She was asleep before I began. Even the thought of my head rubs put her out.

I was wide-awake, but it wasn't the coffee. It was everything on my plate the next day that made me anxious.

I had to get my son to school in the morning. I had writing deadlines to meet before going into work. I was stressed, had many mysteries to solve, like *Where the heck have I seen that actor from that TV show tonight?*

My brain was drowning. I wasn't going to sleep any time soon, but I had nothing to worry about.

I thought about watching a movie. Or maybe finishing a book I was reading. Maybe I could work on meeting those writing deadlines — that'd be the smartest way to use my time and energy.

I got out of bed without waking my wife and made my way down the hall toward the office.

I passed the office and went to the TV to watch that movie instead. That'd help me sleep. See, I had the power here.

Watching the movie only stimulated my mind. It was this thing about zombie robots from another dominion. Don't judge it. It had a very relevant social commentary. In fact, I found uncanny similarities in this book I was reading about the Dust Bowl of 1930s Middle America. Did you know that, during the "dirty 30s," heavy winds carried dust all the way to the East Coast?

It wasn't long before I switched from the robot movie to the Dust Bowl book. That darned book — it reminded me of the Dust Bowl documentary I recorded on my DVR that I hadn't seen yet, so I set the book down, returned to my TV and cued up the doc. I couldn't stick to one activity. I was wasting time.

I had nothing to worry about. I had the power. I decided not to waste more time. I'd work on meeting those writing deadlines.

I went into my home office and fired up the computer. First things first — I checked my email. I came across some funny videos. Has it occurred to anyone else that people don't really tell jokes anymore? Current events used to bring out the best joke tellers. Now we just send a link to a funny video.

I turned my efforts to an Internet search for breaking news about the decline of good old-fashioned joke telling in America due to the advent of viral videos. Before I could peruse my Google results, I realized I was wasting time again, and more importantly, not getting sleep. I had to get my son to school in the morning. I had those deadlines to meet before going to work. I had to figure out where the heck I'd seen that actor from that TV show I'd watched earlier that night. *Was that guy in the new Bond movie?*

Why'd I drink that coffee? What an idiot. I don't even drink coffee. Not often, anyway. I'd lost the power to sleep. I woke my wife and told her my problem. She wasn't happy, did the whole told-you-so thing, but said she'd give me a head rub to help me fall asleep.

It only helped her fall asleep. I couldn't sleep. I couldn't sleep. I couldn't sleep.

Then I fell asleep. And then my alarm screamed at me to take in the morning. And I couldn't wake up.

Everything between my ears throbbed. My mind was in a fog. My wife was up and out the door, which meant I had to get going, too. I had that kid to get to school, those deadlines to meet, that job to work. If I could just get myself out of bed, my feet would do the rest.

I had nothing to worry about.

Two jammed toes later, I found the kitchen. I opened the cupboard and searched for the coffee, but my head hurt so much, I couldn't see. I let my hand do the rest of the work. *Please, no mousetraps.*

And there it was — the K-Cup coffee box. And also the answer I desperately needed — that actor was in a stupid cereal commercial! My mind could finally rest, but I couldn't rest. Not until I found what I needed. I dug into that K-Cup coffee box for the antidote to my sleepless night…

I'd consumed the last cup of coffee last night.

I really had nothing to worry about.

— *March 2013*

CHAPTER FIVE

Tradition and Nostalgia

The Past Is History

The Stories We Pass Down

As I write this, my last remaining grandparent, my paternal grandmother, is in critical condition on her 94th birthday. Grandma Picarella might not make it out of the hospital alive.

When my paternal grandfather died—the first of my grandparents to pass, I regretted not knowing more about him, so I made it a point to get to know my other grandparents better.

I spent hours of one-on-one time with each grandparent, listening to the stories of their lives and of the people around them. They told me many stories—some new, some I'd heard before and some that couldn't possibly be true, but were fun to hear anyway.

My maternal grandmother, Grandma Balsamo, once told me the account of when she was a child and swallowed so much bubble gum that bubble gum bubbles inflated from her belly button. That's right, her belly blew bubbles.

Speaking of belly buttons, my Grandpa Picarella once told me the *true* story of how we get our belly buttons. Before God sends us down to Earth, he lines everyone up on a cloud in Heaven and walks down the line sticking his finger into each belly and twisting a belly button into the skin, saying, "You're done... You're done... You're done." Evidently, that's the finishing touch on us humans before we're born. I still wonder at what point we get the umbilical cord.

Grandma Picarella tells the tale of how she was blessed with a baby boy — my dad. She and my grandfather ate broccoli — lots of broccoli. When she wanted a girl (my aunt), she cut the broccoli out of her diet and, since she cooked the meals, out of my grandfather's diet, too. And *voila!* A girl was born. Broccoli — that's the scientific truth. Go ahead and look it up.

Family members have told some *really* true stories that I'm not at liberty to tell in my column. Here they are anyway:

THERE *Is* NO MAFIA

I've heard the family's Mafia stories, which I'm told are all "just stories" because "the Mafia doesn't *really* exist." I know some fellow Italian-Americans who hate when their heritage is immediately related to the mob, but I'm told that my family is what it is — for better or for worse — because of its Mafia ties. I'm just excited to have one other thing that brings me even closer to *The Godfather* movies.

NAZIS AND WAR

Then there are the anecdotes of Grandpa Picarella in World War II. I have his Nazi pins that, I would later learn, he took off dead German soldiers.

So that's why he had those swastika pins, I thought after hearing the stories behind them. I guess my grandfather wasn't a Nazi after all. That's good to know.

My grandpa traveled home from the war on the Queen Mary and he carved his name into a rail on the ship, but when I visited the ship a couple of years ago, I couldn't find his name.

They probably thought the ship would appear classier to visitors if it wasn't all carved up like a rest-stop bathroom.

Legends of Larry and Mary

As Halloween approaches, I remember scary stories that I'm told were passed down through the generations.

There's the story of the Larry Monster. The *larry*, as some of you may or may not know, is the latrine. When my family would go camping, us kids were warned that, if we dared leave the tent in the middle of the night to use the bathroom, we risked bumping into the Larry Monster, a nasty, stinky blob that resides in the latrine and comes out to suck children in for visiting his lair when they're supposed to be in their tent with their parents.

A bladder explosion might be less painful than a possible run-in with the Larry Monster. My parents would tell me, "Go to the bathroom before bedtime like we always tell you to do, and you won't have to worry about running into him." But seriously, what fun would that be?

There was also the legend of Bloody Mary, which always came up around Halloween time. A long-lost aunt of mine named Mary had killed herself in the bathroom of her home because she had married the wrong man. In those times, divorce was out of the question. Evidently suicide wasn't so good either, because Bloody Mary was forced to roam the Earth endlessly as a ghost.

OK, so the story goes: If you go into your own bathroom, turn off all the lights and say "Bloody Mary" three times in a row, you'll see the apparition of this long-gone aunt of mine, Mary, appear in the mirror. Silly, right? Pretty simple process, right?

I still don't have the guts to try.

SLEIGH RIDE

My dad tells the story of riding in Santa Claus's sleigh as a boy. He told my siblings and me that Santa had never taken anyone in his sleigh before or since — not even Martha Claus, Santa's wife.

Yup, only my dad has ridden in Santa's sleigh. Of course, my son says otherwise — only *his* dad has ridden in that sleigh. There's a story I can believe.

WHERE BABIES COME FROM

My son has already come up with his own story. It's the account of his birth. When he was ready to come out of his mommy's tummy, Mommy lifted her shirt and launched him out of her belly button (what's with all the belly buttons?) and into the air. The kid hit the floor and slid down a hallway like a hockey puck. At the other side of the room, the doctor caught my son with a baseball mitt before he hit the wall. Then the doctor looked him over and said to Mommy and Daddy, "Here's your baby."

My son is so dramatic. As if the doctor would have a baseball mitt. He really used a hockey glove, which goes a lot better with the whole sliding-down-a-hallway-like-a-hockey-puck bit.

BACK TO THE BEGINNING

OK, so I began this column by writing about my dying grandmother and how I wished I knew her better, and how I got to know my living grandparents better by listening to their stories, and then I launched into all these legends that I remember hearing from my grandparents and other family members when I was a kid.

Most of these stories have little to do with my grandparents or other family members, but then again, they have everything to do with them, because of how these people told me the stories. They are stories that preserve the character of my grandparents and my family. And that's more precious to me than just plain old history.

— *October 2007*

White Men Can't Dance

I'm in the sixth grade. It's a birthday party. Music (what would be referred to today as a bad '80s mixtape) blasts through a dual-cassette stereo with a turntable and two big speakers. *She* comes to me with the sweetest smile, one that's loaded down with innocence. She's wearing that incredible dress she wore for her yearbook picture. Wow!

She begs me to dance — only she doesn't say a word. Her innocent smile says it all. She wants me to invite her to the dance floor.

Fat chance. As they say, "white men can't dance," and that's certainly the case for me when it comes dancing to anything but slow songs.

I hate dancing. I don't get it. Basketball: make the most baskets. Baseball: hit the ball. Boxing: knock the other guy down. Dancing: bounce, jump, wiggle…make a fool of yourself to impress a girl? I just don't get it.

I come to the dance floor with what good dancers call the "white man's overbite," and I have no moves, except for left foot in, left foot out, right foot in, right foot out. It's far from cool.

A slow song plays. That's when I ask her to dance. I understand this kind of dancing. It's intimate. It's romantic. The two of us can talk without screaming at each other.

"I didn't come here for the music," I finally say in her ear. "I came here for you."

It seems to work. We step out back for some privacy, away from our friends, away from party chaperones. We share a glass of punch, and I try to make my move toward steady dating. The wind rises and she shivers. Before I know it, we're back inside the heated house, and all eyes are on me and my terrible dance moves again.

I have no technique. I have no rhythm. I have no business dancing. It wouldn't be so bad if I at least *thought* I was good.

My shirt soaks up the sweat on my back. The cotton sticks to my skin. Massive amounts of sixth-grader cologne and perfume makes my head ache. My feet hurt. I'm tired. I still haven't asked the girl out. The Beastie Boys sing that I gotta fight for my right to party. I'm fighting for my right not to get kicked out of the party.

All this grief because, two months prior, my sixth-grade teacher "treated" our class to square dance lessons in the cafeteria. We learned to promenade and step like thunder, do-si-do and swing right under. Square dancing was a lesson in culture, to be educational, healthy and fun. This was a horrible idea.

But had it not been for the square dancing, I never would've gotten so close to the girl dancing to my right. Had it not been for our closeness, she never would've invited me to the party. Had I not gone to the party, the two of us never would've "danced." And had we not "danced," I never would've had the chance to ask her to go steady, which I ended up doing later that night. I figured, since I already felt humiliated by my dance moves, things couldn't get any worse. So I took a shot and asked her out. And it paid off.

That girl was my first steady girlfriend. And everything I gained from that relationship helped me make better choices toward a second relationship, and ditto toward the relationship after that, which eventually led me toward the choosing of the woman I now call my wife.

I'm in the 32nd year of my life. It's an engagement party for a friend. Music (what would be referred to today as a bad '80s mixtape and was actually labeled as such on someone's iPod) blasts through a 5.1 digital surround-sound system. My wife comes to me with the sweetest smile, one that's loaded down with innocence. She's wearing that incredible dress she wore for her bridal shower. Wow!

She begs me to dance — she comes right out and asks, because married women don't hold anything back.

I've been married almost ten years. I've been a dad for six. My wife and I are officially domesticated.

So how is it that I still have to dance to impress a girl?

—*June 2009*

FAMILY NEWS IN BRIEF

TOOTSIE ROLL SWIPER AT LARGE

A five-pound bag of Tootsie Rolls that my wife set aside for trick-or-treaters last week went missing on Sunday. My parents reported a similar incident a few weeks earlier when we paid a visit. "We had a 16-ounce bag of Tootsie Rolls that just disappeared, and we have no idea who could've taken them," said my mom. "Strange — we haven't had missing Tootsie Rolls since my son Mike left home years ago." Sources reported no specific information about this Tootsie Roll Swiper at large. Authorities suggest that, if you already bought Tootsie Rolls for trick-or-treaters this Halloween, you turn your supply over as a means to avoid a likely run-in with the deadly Swiper himself. Email Michael Picarella at michael.picarella@gmail.com, and he'll gladly take your Tootsie Rolls off your hands.

BELOVED FAX MACHINE DIES AT FIVE

On the night of Friday, June 13th, my fax machine of five years died in its sleep. I'd recently used it during the day to fax an important document to my insurance company. Afterward, I shut the machine down for the night, and the next day when I turned it on, it showed signs of illness, and then it passed away. "Vvvvv-tch-vvvvvvv-tch-vvv," said the machine just before its death, followed by what bystanders called a dreadful "blop." Memorial services were held in my backyard at the Picarella Memorial Trash Can. After my wife's heartfelt eulogy, my four-year-old son fired a two-water-gun salute. "We've all had a chance to remember the good times we had with that fax machine, but we've had to move on," my wife said in a statement last week. "We bought a fax/scanner/printer/copier all-in-one machine, and life is good again."

FRIEND LOST OVER DINNER-TAB FEUD

Yesterday, a family friend mailed my father an anonymous $70 check, enough to cover a dinner tab from 20 years earlier. The 1989 dinner, according to the family friend, was supposed to be *his* treat, not my father's, but my father wouldn't let him pay. "It was my idea to go to dinner in the first place," the family friend said. "The fact that he would disguise a visit to the cashier as a trip to the restroom was low down." Analysts said the kind gesture of paying the tab — maybe an attempt to show affection for the fellow man — clearly backfired when a feud over who'd pay for a few steak dinners at a neighborhood Sizzler turned into a war of silence that's lasted two decades. My father shredded the $70 check he recently received. Some feuds, experts suggest, never end.

Pumpkin Candies

I HAVE A FEELING MY WIFE IS OUT TO GET ME.

She was all of 39 years old when she decided she didn't want to be 40. So she punishes me.

SUSPICIONS

What is she looking for? I haven't done anything wrong. Unless she says so. She follows me to the garage, to the mailbox and even down the hall. She tries to follow me into the bathroom. She digs through our closets, under the bed, through my dirty laundry. She calls my mom and talks secretively to her.

"What do you think I've done?" I finally ask her.

"I'm not spying on you or looking for anything," she says. "I'm not doing anything."

I bring up specific instances. She denies it all. I tell her to stop. She says she isn't doing anything.

"But you are," I say.

She says she isn't doing anything.

That's how arguments go in our house.

A HISTORY

During Halloween time when I was around eight years old, I ate so many pumpkin candies, I made myself sick. My stomach rejected these pumpkin candies — more accurately, my stomach *projected* these pumpkin candies. This happened in church. Needless to say, the people in front of me were less than thrilled.

My love for the sweet Mellowcreme candy wasn't immediate. At about age four, when first introduced to pumpkin candies (small, pumpkin-shaped confections made mostly from corn syrup, honey, wax and sugar, and tasting like candy corn), I didn't want to eat them. I wanted to draw faces on them and put them up as decorations for Halloween.

Then I made the mistake of taking a bite. Yum. But even at such an early age, when the stomach can practically take any dose of candy and not get upset, my stomach hurt after only two or three bags. What made matters worse was I had to have more, the same effect I imagine nicotine has on smokers.

During my childhood, my mother would fill up a glass pumpkin jar with pumpkin candies every October. I'd quickly gobble those babies down. After my churchgoing incident with the pumpkin candies, I learned to manage my pumpkin candy intake. I knew my limit — sort of.

I came close to repeating the church disaster many times, but I have to say, as an adult, I've never come close to eating too much. If I stick to one bag every Halloween season, I'll be fine.

I just can't give them up. Each bite of those candies gives me a rush of Halloween nostalgia. Those childhood days of

Halloween are some of the highlights of my life. Halloween, you see, is my favorite time of year. It's a time of magic, of make-believe, of becoming someone else (or some*thing* else). It's the mystery and excitement of seeing others' costumes, of seeing how others respond to yours. It's about giving and getting candy, scaring and getting scared. You laugh, you scream, you run, you dream. You play tricks and get tricked. It's a heck of a ride.

With that first bite of the sweet Mellowcreme each year comes a burst of Halloween memories: my earliest experience trick-or-treating without adults, going into inventive haunted house walk-throughs, including that one house that might've actually been haunted. The second bite of the candy now makes me sick.

"Why is this happening?" I asked during the last few Halloween seasons of pumpkin-candy consumption. Last year, I considered throwing out my bag of candies after eating only two pieces.

My wife, unsupportive as she is, told me that throwing out the candy puts me on the right track. Can you believe that? They're bad for my stomach, she said, bad for my diet (funny, I don't have one), bad for my teeth. And "Pumpkin candies are just gross," she added. My wife just doesn't want me to be happy.

BACK TO THE "SNEAK" PIT

I catch my wife at the trashcan with my bag of pumpkin candies.

"What are you doing?" I ask.

"Throwing these out," she answers. "I'm just trying to make you healthy."

I'm touched to learn of her concern for me. Really. I tell her I don't need the pumpkin candies anymore, that they make me sick, that the memories are all reruns anyway.

But that night, I can't help it. I sneak out to the trashcan in search of that bag of magic she threw out, not unlike the way Dr. Frankenstein ventured into the graveyard to find a body for his monster. This parallel makes me consider the damage I might cause — every Frankenstein story I've seen ended terribly for Dr. Frankenstein.

So I turn around before I open the can to retrieve my candies. I go back to my wife to confess my sins.

And I catch her.

Ah ha, my wife isn't out to get me. As she eats from the bag she never threw out, I learn that, all along, she was out to get my pumpkin candies!

— *September 2012*

The "Friday the 13th" Incident

MY WIFE AND FOUR-YEAR-OLD SON THINK I'M CRAZY.

Today is Friday the 13th, a day that rains bad luck on some people. I don't use my air conditioning or drive my car, for fear they'll break down in episodes of misfortune. I certainly don't want to "accidentally" turn up dead.

So this Friday the 13th, I'm staying clear of bad news and bad luck. I'll be tucked away in the back of my bedroom closet with the door locked.

OK, so I'm a little superstitious. But I have reason to be superstitious.

It all started when I was about eight years old. My best friend and I learned about the *Friday the 13th* films, where Jason Voorhees, the supernatural slayer who wears a white (sometimes blood-red) hockey mask, kills people with his machete. The older neighborhood kids told my friend and me that little kids like us couldn't see the movies because we'd be too scared, which basically meant that we *had* to get a hold of these movies somehow and watch them.

So my friend and I went to the local video store and tried to rent all four films (a collection that's since grown). The man behind the counter wouldn't rent the R-rated videos to us. So we did what any good youths would do. We lied.

I led the fibbing with a story about how my parents asked me to come down and rent the movies for their personal viewing. I felt terrible lying, but I was really good at it.

Evidently, I wasn't good enough because the plan didn't work. Maybe that was a sign that we should've given up before we got into trouble, but we didn't give up. We spent the rest of the day visiting all the video stores in town in search of a clerk who would rent us the films.

Just when we were about to give up, because it was getting late and the monsters would soon come out to eat us, we found someone who would rent us the movies. At Apple Video, we were short one cent at the register, which was another sign telling us not to rent the videos, then the guy threw in a penny from the "leave a penny, take a penny" basket, and we were home free.

With the *Friday the 13th* movies in hand, we went straight to our secret hideaway, our fort, conveniently located in my best friend's backyard just under his bedroom window. It was a convenient location because we were able to drop an extension cord down from his room into our fort, and plug in a VCR and TV inside, so we could view the movies without our parents knowing.

I called home and asked if I could spend the night at my friend's house. I got permission, and we started our *Friday the 13th* marathon. The films knocked us over the head with blood and guts and over-the-top brutal imagery.

It was great!

We loved the movies so much that we had to have more, so the next day we went back to our R-rated video connection and rented *Nightmare on Elm Street*, the *Halloween* movies, and *The Texas Chain Saw Massacre*.

As we smuggled the videos back to our fort, my best friend and I marveled at how we were able to rent R-rated videos without getting caught.

Then we got caught. We'd pushed our luck. My parents happened to be driving by and found us with the sack of movies. They took the movies back to the video store and told the clerk that I couldn't rent movies there ever again, not even *Sesame Street*, and told me I couldn't spend the night in the fort anymore either.

I later came to realize why I got busted. I compared the whole experience to a common algebra equation. The way I figured it, my friend and I were instantly doomed when we rented R-rated movies (a negative), but because we rented *Friday the 13th* (a second negative, as the film relates to a day filled with bad luck), we ended up with two negatives, and two negatives make a positive, so we could've walked away clean.

But then we rented other R-rated movies (a negative). We had no other negative to make a positive. That's why we got busted.

OK, so maybe my wife and four-year-old son have good reason to think I'm going crazy. Nevertheless, you can bet that today, Friday the 13th (a negative), I'll still be tucked away in the back of my closet where no bad luck can attack me. I'll be sitting under a ladder (a second negative) in front of the TV, watching the *Friday the 13th* movies (a third negative) and breaking mirrors (a fourth negative).

Four negatives make a double positive. I hope it's enough to make it to midnight.

—June 2008

BITS FROM THE 'BURBS

GOING BACK

It isn't the way it used to be. Maybe it never was.

A SIGN OF TOUGH TIMES

It's easy during tough times like these to derail emotionally, get depressed, lose focus due to overwhelming despair, and miss the things in life that really count. The other day, while driving south on Interstate 5 into Orange County, I drove past Disneyland and forgot to point out to my family, using my usual Disneyland Monorail announcer voice, the site of the majestic Matterhorn Mountain. After we went by, my wife asked if I was OK, if I was working too hard. This was a telling sign that some fun is needed in my life. That or someone pulled a fast one on me and moved the mountain.

NO PEEKING

Years ago, my son and I started a tradition of watching Charlie Chaplin films every Sunday, but we haven't done that in a long time, so I thought I'd surprise my boy, now six, with one of our favorites, *Modern Times*. "Don't look," I said, "or no surprise for you." The kid couldn't wait. "A Chaplin film?" he sulked when he saw it. "Ah, Dad, I *did* peek. No surprise for me, right?" I told him I'd let it slide this time. "But Daddy, I don't like gray movies anymore. I like detail."

Egg Cheaters

I WON'T BE PARTICIPATING IN THE FAMILY EASTER Egg Hunt and Barbecue Eggstravaganza this year.

I won't participate because every year the group elects me to barbecue the food, and I'm sick of doing it.

Another reason I won't participate is because I just don't enjoy bugs eating me alive.

And I suppose another reason I won't participate is because I'm not allowed back for what I did last year.

My five-year-old son has represented my immediate family in the annual egg hunt for the past three years, but he's neglected to take home the first-place prize.

I like to win, so I did my best to encourage my boy.

"Do you really think second place is any better than last place?" I'd say to him. "Win first-place prize or run laps around the park."

My wife thinks I'm too hard on the kid. "The egg hunt is supposed to be fun," she'd say, "not work."

Two years ago, during the Great Easter Egg Hunt of '07, one of the parents expertly coached his little egg hunter to the biggest victory in the history of the event.

In other words, the father/son duo cheated.

"I got the most eggs ever, I win the big basket, candy, candy, candy!" the kid yelled as he collected first-place prize, a massive, overweight gift basket of Easter goodies.

You could call my son's second-place gift basket "easier to carry." My wife was thrilled — she misses the point of competition.

Cheater Kid taunted my son: "My basket's bigger than yours."

My son, who knew the kid cheated, took the high ground and didn't sock the boy in the mouth. Instead he congratulated him. It was an honorable move.

I have no shame. "You cheated!" I screamed to the dad, who, standing there in his dorky white tennis shoes, laughed and denied the charge.

Everybody told me to calm down, said I was upset over a silly, irrelevant little egg hunt. Then they contacted the media and reported Cheater Kid's record-breaking victory.

As I cooked everyone's food that year, I plotted how I'd get even in '08.

Each year, the Great Egg Hunt rewards young hunters who find the majority of the 100 plastic eggs that we parents hide before the event. The kid who won the Great Easter Egg Hunt of '07 collected 69 eggs that year — thanks to his cheating dad.

So, following the '07 event, I went to the store and bought 600 plastic eggs and an Easter basket big enough to hold all 600. During the Great Easter Egg Hunt of '08, while the kids were busy hunting and the parents were busy watching, my son and I would meet in a secluded area of the park, and I'd smuggle the 600 eggs from my car into my kid's basket. No other hunter would be able to compete with my boy when it came time to count eggs.

That day, before the hunt, I went to great lengths to prove to everyone that I wasn't sore about the previous year's incident. I bought quality meats to barbecue instead of the usual hot dogs. I even complimented Cheater Dad's brand-new dorky white tennis shoes. I conversed with him, laughed with him...I told him I thought his kid would break the egg-hunt record again.

When the kids were off and hunting, I tiptoed away from the group and over to my car. I couldn't wait to see Cheater Dad's face as my son dumped out his 600 eggs. I even brought my video camera so I could capture the scene on tape for repeat viewings.

I got to my car, disarmed it, popped the trunk...and discovered that my wife had removed the 600 eggs and hid them with the others. She thought the hunt would be better for the kids if they had more eggs to find.

So I trudged back to the egg-hunting grounds and watched Cheater Dad and his cheater kid steal another first-place prize.

Then I fired up the barbecue.

And I burned everyone's food.

— *April 2009*

Waste a Wish

It all started in 1982 when I was six years old. I got into trouble and had to take a half-hour time-out.

I remember thinking that a half-hour meant an hour and a half, assuming that "half" was in addition to the hour, so when I sat down on the couch to do my stretch of time, I knew I was in for a long haul.

The first five minutes of my sentence were torture. After 15 minutes "in the joint," I was convinced that I'd be old and gray before my time-out expired. Each minute felt like a decade, even though, at six, I hadn't yet experienced a decade.

I wished that time would speed up. I knew it was unlikely that my wish would come true, but I figured wishing couldn't hurt.

After 20 minutes, time wasn't moving any faster, and it seemed like the clock was ridiculing me, saying, "You think that long wait for Christmas morning and presents took forever? You ain't seen nothin' yet, pal."

So I verbalized my wish out loud and clear — I didn't care who heard me.

Before I knew it, my half-hour time-out was over, and the wait wasn't all that bad, especially since I was expecting to be "put away" for an hour and a half. I was convinced that my wish to speed up time had come true.

Years later, when I was 15, I bought a beat-up old truck, with plans to rebuild it before I got my driver's license on my 16th birthday.

That 15th year of life was the longest year ever. I came to that conclusion after only the first month. I was extremely anxious to drive, and the massive undertaking of rebuilding a vehicle from the frame up, which was as much fun as sorting through a massive stack of lawn trimmings and organizing the blades of grass by their height, didn't help speed up time.

After three months of work on my truck, I decided I wouldn't live long enough to experience my 16th birthday, and I'd certainly never see my little automobile project completed, so just as I'd done in that time-out when I was six, I wished out loud for time to speed up.

Guess what? It worked. In no time, I was 16 years old with my driver's license in hand, I was finished with my truck, and I was driving it. Life was great.

Unfortunately, it never occurred to me to test my wishing powers on something other than speeding up time. Had I been conscious of my abilities, I might've asked for something more worthy, like a million dollars or a fourth *Godfather* film in the franchise. Instead, at 18 years of age, I wasted another precious wish.

Before I started college, I wished that the four years ahead of me would race by. Believe it or not, my college years did just that.

After graduation, time continued moving at a fast pace. I met a girl, we got married, we bought a house...pretty soon, I got to thinking that time was moving a little too fast. So I made a wish to slow down time.

Nothing happened.

I guess you're only granted three wishes at birth, and I wasted all three of mine before I was 30.

Time is still fleeting. Just last week, my son started kindergarten. I could swear he was born only yesterday.

— *August 2008*

More Family News in Brief

A Family Man Reflects on Father's Day

Father's Day is a great day to sit in your favorite chair wearing your favorite pajamas and reflect. I did plenty of reflecting this year with a close friend who plans to get married and start a family very soon. "Some of the years as a family man go by really fast," I warned him. He nodded as if he'd heard this before, and as if he believed it. "But some of the afternoons last an eternity." My friend nodded and decided not to talk to me about marriage and kids anymore.

Hot Pursuit Goes Three Hours

In a chase that lasted three hours and spanned the distance of ten football fields but within the confines of a local single-family dwelling, my father-in-law finally captured my five-year-old son in the outskirts of the living room, and tickled the boy into an uncontrollable laughter. "I just didn't want to be tickled." my son said after the fact. "So I ran." According to Grandpa, grandparents have been tickling their grandchildren for generations, and they'll hunt those little ones down at any cost to produce that all-important involuntary laughter and wriggling. My son's belly still hurts from laughing as hard as he did.

New Year's Hopes and Dreams
at an All-Time High

It's that time of year to hope and dream, and a new study shows that hopes and dreams have reached record levels as 2009 comes to a close. According to a local dream authority, tough times bring out more hopes and more dreams in even the most negative people. "Unemployment rates have been hitting record levels and economic recovery seems as far into the future as hover boards," the source said. "But it's in times like these that hopes and dreams are all we have to get us through." According to insiders, ten percent of all dreams in this world come true. "That stated," one expert said, "it's simple mathematics. When you've got more people dreaming and making wishes and having hope, then you've got more people having dreams that come true. How can you not take that action?" My family figured our odds and placed all bets on hope. Thankfully, there won't be some bookie named "Ice Pick Nicky" coming to collect if our dreams aren't winners.

What's in the Basket?

I COULDN'T FIGURE OUT WHAT TO PUT IN MY NINE-year-old son's Easter basket this year. What I mean is — the Easter Bunny fills up his basket with goodies, but my wife and I like to put something in there from us.

But what? It had to be good, but nothing to spoil the kid. After all, Easter isn't about gifts. Not huge ones, anyway.

I remember the year I learned about greed. I was about my son's age. My mom said she'd found the ultimate Easter gift for me, one that I'd particularly love.

I was intrigued. A gift I specifically would appreciate? My mom talked about it for weeks. I remember thinking it couldn't have been all *that* good.

It wasn't. It was a light-up skeleton pen. I think I let out an "Ahhhhh, what the —' when I saw it in my basket on Easter morning, even though I loved to draw and I adored anything to do with monsters, skeletons and ghouls. Maybe my mom's setup led me to believe it'd be something like a new wing in the house...just for me, with an indoor swimming pool and a skate park.

It took me a full minute after seeing the pen before I could fake excitement. I hoped my mom didn't catch my initial disappointment. She was so eager for me to receive that gift. My plan was to never let her find out what I really thought.

"This is the best gift ever," I lied. "I love it more than Christmas."

I reminded her daily how highly I thought of the pen, went out of my way to use it in front of her.

After spring break, when I went back to school, one of my friends, Joey, bragged about the motorcycle he got for Easter.

"You got a pen?" Joey asked as if I were kidding. "You gotta tell your parents who's boss."

He put me through a "Here's how you get good things" boot camp. I learned to ask for fast-food money instead of sitting down with my family for meals. I learned to leave my room so messy that my mom would have no choice but to clean it up for me. I learned that saying thank you was as bad as telling my parents I didn't need anything else from them.

I went along with Joey, but I'd never treat my parents with such disrespect. However, at Joey's house, I watched how his tactics pleased his parents. Joey got what he wanted, and his mom and dad were thrilled to spoil him. His parents were happy like my mom was happy to give me that skeleton pen.

Maybe I could please my parents by telling them to get me a motorcycle. *I'd* be happy.

I found my mom in the kitchen. Joey tagged along to witness my metamorphosis.

"Hey, Mom," I began. "Um... do you remember where you got that pen? Joey wants one, too."

I just couldn't do it. I tried. I really tried, but I couldn't be greedier than I already felt. Joey punched me in the arm, reminding me to stick to the plan. I couldn't, so Joey did it for me, telling my mom she owed me a motorcycle after insulting me with that lame pen.

I was going kill Joey, but first I ran up to my room to hide.

After my mom sent Joey home, she came up to talk to me. I hoped my bedcovers, having shielded me from numerous closet monsters in the past, would surely save me from facing a disappointed, hurt mother.

Could you believe it? The covers didn't protect me. My mom talked right through the sheets. I begged for forgiveness, promised I'd never be greedy again.

My mom forgave me.

This year, as I loaded up on stuff for my son's Easter basket, I thought about that promise. I was acting greedy all over again. I put all the stuff back on the shelf, save a few items.

On Easter day, my son's tiny, almost empty basket looked great. It did. There was plenty in there. Well, it wasn't about quantity. It was about quality. By quality, I mean it was the thought that counted.

Evidently, it was the thought that counted. My son couldn't have been happier if we gave him a new wing in the house...just for him, with an indoor swimming pool and a skate park. He only wanted us to hide more eggs for him to find.

We did egg hunts all day. That night, my son finally confessed.

"Daddy," he said, "I have to admit — I was hoping the Easter Bunny would've hid my basket a little better. I'm nine years old now and I can—""You're a great kid," I interrupted. "If I could get you a motorcycle for Easter, I would."

My son assured me that he didn't need a motorcycle.

"That's a relief," I said. "Because the second you feel we owe you a motorcycle, you get nothing."

— *April 2013*

Memorial Daze

I HAVE WARM MEMORIES OF MEMORIAL DAY WEEK-ends past.

During a recent phone call with my dad, he said he had some memories, too — none of them warm.

He recalled the days when he and my mom were still married and hosted Memorial Day gatherings at our house. The two of them would rise before the sun on the Saturday morning of Memorial Day weekend and prepare.

My mom spent the morning in the kitchen cooking massive amounts of food that never seemed to fit into our two refrigerators. She spent the entire afternoon cleaning what we kids thought was an already immaculate house. It wasn't just a job, she'd say, but a family adventure.

My dad did the yard work, cleaned the pool and set up the dining arrangements out back. He was also in charge of commanding us kids to keep quiet. "I can't concentrate on my work," he'd scream as he mowed the lawn.

According to my dad, our guests never had to do anything but show up, eat and relax.

"But when we went to their houses," he said, "we were expected to bring a salad or a dessert, a set of bowls of some sort or an ice cream maker or extra dishes or a small table for the kids — we'd stuff the trunk of the car. I used to wonder why we were going to their houses when I was bringing half of my house and doing half the work."

My dad said family gatherings became more and more of a nuisance as the years passed.

"I had an aunt who had to cut everything in half," he said. "She'd cut the cannoli in half, cheeses in half, a piece of salami in half — she'd even cut halves of sandwiches in half. She'd come over, we'd have everything prepared, and she'd go into the refrigerator, pull out the food and start cutting it in half."

I don't remember that, but I do recall games of Marco Polo in the pool with all my cousins, competing in our annual family badminton tournament and playing pin the tail on my kid brother.

I also remember one particular Memorial Day barbecue at our house when one of my aunts spent the better part of the afternoon throwing coins into the pool for us kids to fetch. By nightfall, we'd filled three empty pickle jars with the money we gathered. My dad recalled that particular incident but, as before, not as fondly as I did.

What I don't remember, he said, was that, just before everyone went home, one of my uncles emptied our pickle jars of coins back into the pool. My dad spent the rest of the evening at my uncle's throat. My uncle spent the rest of the evening fetching the coins out of the pool.

"You don't remember how bad it was," my dad told me. "You were too young."

He remembered the steaks that burned, the pool flotation devices that flattened and the screaming youngsters who didn't want to go home.

What is past is prologue, unless we choose to remember the things we don't want to repeat. My father said he "experienced" all those Memorial Day gatherings so that I might avoid them when it came time for me to serve my tour of suburban dad duty. I've always tried to make my dad proud.

This Saturday, my wife, five-year-old son and I are hosting a Memorial Day barbecue for friends. We did everything beforehand so that our guests don't have to do anything but show up, eat and relax. On Sunday, we're going to a family barbecue at someone else's house. My wife said we only have to make a salad and bring dessert. And we have to bring some dishes and our big fruit bowl. And toys for the kids. And charcoal for the barbecue. And our barbecue.

While I may have failed to learn from family men like my father, who fell during the Memorial Day gatherings of their time, I will never forget the real heroes who died for this country to protect our right to freely repeat Memorial Day weekend blunders.

— May 2009

MORE BITS FROM THE 'BURBS

HALLOWEEN'S ALMOST HERE

My six-year-old son has seen *It's the Great Pumpkin, Charlie Brown* 3,000 times. It's a tradition. After a recent viewing, he said, "Daddy, it's Halloween time — we better get ready for 'tricks or treats.'" I said, "We still have two weeks." He said, "Then we better hurry and get pumpkins and candy and our costumes — " I cut him off. "We have plenty of time, son." So he asked, "Then can we watch *It's the Great Pumpkin, Charlie Brown* again?" I said, "No, we have only two weeks — we better hurry and get pumpkins and candy…"

FALL

You know it's fall when the air gets cold, the wind blows and the leaves color the ground yellow and orange. As a kid, I loved to jump and roll around in the big piles of leaves. So I went to Walmart and, believe it or not, they didn't have leaves for sale.

TURKEY TV

Nothing brings in the holiday season like the Macy's Thanksgiving Parade. I'd watch the whole parade if there wasn't so much singing and dancing. And so many marching bands. And all that nonsensical banter from the commentators. And then those commercials. And it's such a long parade. And everything moves so slowly. I like the balloons.

Live to Eat

I RECENTLY UNDERWENT HEART SURGERY. DURING most of my recovery up until now, I haven't had much of an appetite. However, as I begin to phase out the medication and return to my normal self, my hunger for food is becoming strong. In fact, my hunger is so strong that I feel I can eat all day long. I'm starving, and I can use a large meal.

I think of my Grandma Picarella and my maternal grand-mother, Grandma Balsamo. These two women never left the kitchen, as far as I know, and made enough food on a given day to feed all the troops overseas — on both sides of the war. Both of my grandmothers claimed the phrase, "Most people eat to live; Italians live to eat." And it was their mission to cook.

As a kid, I remember several occasions when my siblings and I spent the night at Grandma Picarella's house. We'd wake up the next day to the smell of homemade meat sauce cooking. In the kitchen, Grandma would be preparing meat sauce for dinner that evening and making breakfast.

Breakfast wasn't just eggs and bacon. Breakfast was enough food to make the Biltmore Hotel's buffet look like a two-year-old's snack. I'd kill myself trying to finish my first serving, and then Grandma would say, "Eat. There's plenty more."

"I can't eat any more, Grandma," I'd say. "I'm stuffed."

"What's the matter? You don't like my food? Eat. I can't save this."

Grandma would tell me how I needed to eat because I was a "growing boy," and that I didn't want to be "skin and bones because the girls like big and strong men."

Italian guilt never worked on me. I ate only two or three more plates of food.

Stuffed for the remainder of the day, most of us would retire into the living room or backyard to rest and digest. Grandma would clean up the breakfast dishes, and then she'd get started on lunch.

While preparing the mid-day meal, Grandma would offer up pizzelles (Italian cookies) that she'd made. We kids — not able to fit even two more morsels of food into our bel-lies — would always say, "No thanks." The adults knew better. They just ate the cookies to avoid unnecessary servings of Italian guilt. Eventually, the rest of us took the cookies, too.

Lunch followed soon after. A variety of sandwiches lined the kitchen counters like the Macy's Parade floats line the streets of New York on Thanksgiving Day. You ordered your sandwiches as you would at an Italian football wedding where someone calls out sandwich orders to another person near a cooler of sandwiches, and that person would throw the sandwiches across the room to the order-taker:

"Dominic, I'll take a capicola sandwich. Throw over a salami and provolone." *Swish*, the sandwiches would fly through the air like footballs over the guests' heads. Quite a scene.

Lunch always included side dishes of all sorts. By the end of the meal, you always wondered where you found room in your stomach to store so much food. After stuffing ourselves, we'd again retire to the living room or backyard to rest and digest.

Grandma would clean up the lunch dishes. Then she'd start dinner.

Dinner was a big deal, especially if it was a Sunday dinner. Sunday dinner always started around three p.m. and could involve neighbors and friends.

Grandpa Balsamo used to open up his home to practically anyone on Sundays. He actually left the doors open and invited pedestrians in for dinner. Sometimes strangers would come in for dinner. My grandma always had plenty of food. Believe me.

Dinner usually kicked off with the antipasto, which includes cheeses, raw or marinated vegetables, cold cuts and cured meats such as prosciutto — somewhat of a meal in itself.

Next came the macaroni. For those who think I'm talking about macaroni and cheese, let me explain: Macaroni is what most people call "pasta" with meat sauce or marinara sauce. I never heard the word "pasta" until I was about six years old, so I still call it macaroni. Some of my family members still don't talk with each other because of arguments from 20 years ago about whether it's called macaroni or pasta.

Following the macaroni was usually sausage and meatballs or pork or veal — some sort of meat dish, and then came the salad prepared with homemade oil-and-vinegar dressing.

After that, the fruit and nuts rolled in, and then maybe a pastry like cannoli, spumoni ice cream and/or more pizzelles for dessert.

The adults would follow that with coffee with anisette and some biscotti for dipping.

By the time the meal was consumed, the sun had gone down and the party had moved into the living room or the backyard for resting and digesting, allowing everyone to play cards or tell stories. Grandma would still be occupied in the kitchen, cleaning up the dishes and getting prepared for the next day's meals.

The other day, as a means to answer my stomach's calling for massive amounts of nourishment, I cooked up not even half the amount of food my grandmothers would've typically made on a Sunday. It was a ton of food still, and I set out to eat it all.

I didn't make a dent. Anyone wanna come over for three weeks of meals?

— *March 2007*

Fish Sleeps with Luca Brasi

WHEN JOHNNY FONTANE WHIMPERED TO HIS GODFA-ther about his inability to get a part in a movie, Don Vito Corleone, with anger and disappointment in his voice, commanded his godson to act like a man.

"What's the matter with you?" the godfather yelled. "Is this how you turned out? A Hollywood *finocchio* that cries like a woman?"

The character Marlon Brando played in *The Godfather* is the quintessential man; he's tough, he's strong... and he certainly wouldn't cry if he lost a pet.

Last week, while on vacation, my in-laws called with a Sicilian message. They said my five-year-old son's pet fish, Fish E. Fish (aka Tiny Fish), sleeps with Luca Brasi. In other words, so you non-Sicilians and non-*Godfather* lovers can understand, Fish died.

My son wasn't shaken at all.

"He's a man," I told my wife when she asked why our boy wasn't sad.

"But Fish is never going to come back," my wife told our boy, trying to get him to break. "He's gone forever. Don't you feel any sadness?"

"The kid's fine," I said. "Why do you want him to be a baby?"

"It's OK, Mommy," our son said. "I'm not sad."

Ah, some day my son will take over the family business.

I gave Fish a proper burial. I packed his body into a small jewelry box, and buried it in our backyard planter. My son said a few kind words about his former pet, and that was that.

"Is Fish up in Heaven now?" the boy asked as we went inside. "Or do you think he's stuck in traffic?"

"No, he's in Heaven," my wife said. "But he's never coming back. You understand that, right? He's never ever, ever coming back — ever."

My son thought about all those "evers."

"Are you sad now?" my wife asked him.

Just then our son broke into tears.

"Now why did you do that?" I asked my wife. "How's he ever gonna be a man?"

"He's not a baby because he's sad that his pet died," my wife said. "It's OK to be sad and have feelings."

"But he was fine before," I said. "It's like you wanted him to feel bad."

"No, I just don't want him to think he has to hold back his emotions," she said.

I thought about what my wife said, and I tried to find the logic in a growing boy crying about a dead fish. Maybe it was OK that —

"No, it's not OK," I said. "What's the matter with you? Do you want our son to be a Hollywood *finocchio* that cries like a woman?"

Of everyone in my family, I should've been the most emotional over the death of Fish. I took care of Fish. I fed him most of the time, I cleaned his tank, I changed the light in his tank when it went out, I gave him medicine when he was ill...

Just because I'm not wallowing in grief, doesn't mean I don't have feelings for Fish. I have lots of fond memories of him — like when we first brought him home from the pet store and I took pictures of the two of us together for my wallet, or like when I used to try to communicate with him every morning by tapping Morse code on the aquarium glass. Fish and I even joked around with my wife and son when I cleaned the tank. I'd move him to another bowl and pretend he went missing.

Yep, Fish and I had some really great times. Sniff sniff. And I'm sure gonna miss him. Sniff sniff. And there's no way I can bring him back ever, ever again. Ever. WAAAAH!

There's a scene in *The Godfather* where Don Vito Corleone is in an undertaker's place looking over his son's bullet-riddled body. The Don becomes very emotional. Remember? He said, "Look how they massacred my boy." The Godfather practically bawled all over the corpse.

And that's how I justify my tears for Fish.

— *January 2009*

CHAPTER 6

Friends and Fun

"F" Words

Contact? Contact Again!

MY WIFE AND I LIVED IN THE SAN FRANCISCO BAY
Area for many years. When the two of us moved to Southern California in the year 2000, we left several friends
behind.

It's tough to move away from good friends. You see them
every day for years, and then one day you move hundreds of
miles away and they're gone. When I moved to Los Angeles,
I knew I'd have to pay a lot of money on long-distance
phone calls and make a lot of trips up the coast to keep in
touch.

For the past nine years, I've had little luck getting those
friends on the phone. I can't even get in touch with them via
email or social networks like Facebook, and I've only once
been back home to see them. That was for a wedding many
years ago.

My wife and I work long days, we have a five-year-old
son who keeps us very busy, and we spend a considerable
amount of the little spare time we have just trying to stay in
touch with extended family (which is a must or they write
us off). When we do get the chance to call our friends from
back home, we face the unlikely chance of reaching them,
and the likely chance they won't call us back.

Still, I keep trying. It's become my mission to contact a few particular friends who were among my closest buddies back home.

I asked family members how they keep in touch with special people who are hundreds of miles away.

"Well, it's tough," they said. "If they don't call us, we don't call them. We usually lose touch."

Three years ago, I called one of my closest buddies from back home and got a hold of his wife.

"Oh no, you just missed him," she told me. "He's always beating himself up, saying he needs to return your calls. I always tell him that you know his work is crazy and that you know he has a family and new friends and no time to call you back, and I tell him that you totally understand…I'll tell him you called."

I never heard from him.

Around the same time, another one of my closest buddies from back home returned one of my emails from two years previous.

"Sorry I'm just getting back to you now," he wrote. "I'm not one for correspondence. In fact, I really only keep in touch with my mom and dad and a few close friends and some old co-workers and some old friends from school. Don't be offended if I can't keep in touch with you. I probably won't even respond to your response to this response. See ya."

That was it.

That's when destiny stepped in and provided the opportunity I needed to make real contact. I had to get a pacemaker installed in my chest to fix a little problem I had with my heart stopping. My wife emailed the news to friends and family, and I figured I'd certainly receive sympathy calls from my close buddies from back home, if not a visit.

Instead I got emails.

"That's crazy," one of my buddies wrote. "It's times like these that makes you cherish your friends."

"We can't believe you had to get a pacemaker," wrote the wife of another buddy. "We're just shaking our heads."

That was it. Two brief sentences each.

I spent the next year and a half trying to respond to those emails. I called. I emailed. I MySpaced. I Facebooked. No response.

Last year, I ended my efforts.

Yesterday, an old coworker of mine from back home contacted me on MySpace. He said he bumped into my good buddy and his wife (the couple that shook their heads when they heard about my heart surgery). My old coworker said he'd asked the couple if they kept in touch with me.

My buddy told him, "Mike doesn't call anymore."

— *March 2009*

Tower Is a Terror

"YOU WANNA GO ON SOMETHING REALLY FAST AND really scary?" I asked my five-year-old son during a recent trip to Disney's California Adventure theme park. He seemed to think that every ride we rode was too slow and too boring, so I wanted to excite him.

"Yeah," my boy said with enough enthusiasm to make a cooped-up Jack Russell terrier look like an energy-deficient loaf. "I wanna go on something really, really fast and really, really scary." Then my son did what he does when he gets excited — he jumped up and down.

Twilight Zone Tower of Terror is an elevator ride that takes riders to the top of what looks like the Hollywood Tower, and then drops them straight down to the bottom. It was pure, awful, death-defying terror. And we were in line to ride it.

My wife asked if it'd be too scary for our child. I said it couldn't be worse than Splash Mountain or Big Thunder, scary rides the kid had already survived and loved. I gave my wife a smile of confidence, and I was truly confident.

Then I looked to see if there were other five-year-olds in line for the ride because, you know, I didn't want to be the only bad parent with a young one. The youngest kid in line was maybe 24 years old.

As we neared the attraction, we heard riders screaming things like, "I hate this!" and "We're all gonna die!" We saw riders exiting the building with wet pants. My wife asked if this was a water ride. I told her it wasn't.

I excused myself from line to use the restroom. I actually sought out a park employee and asked if it was safe to bring a five-year-old on the Tower of Terror. She said that bringing a five-year-old on the ride was a horrible idea, and very dangerous.

Just before I regained consciousness so I could run back to my family in line and save my son's life, the employee laughed and said she was kidding and that my five-year-old would be fine.

I didn't think this woman was funny. It didn't occur to me until it was far too late that maybe the lady wasn't an employee of the park at all, but in the moment, what she said assured me that everything would be OK.

"This ride is going to be great," I said with renewed enthusiasm as I jumped back in line with my family.

"Is it gonna be really, really fast?" my son asked, eagerly anticipating the horror.

"Yes," I said. "It's going to be more fun than Splash Mountain and Big Thunder put together."

My son jumped up and down — there was that excitement again.

Finally, the line of people we were waiting behind led us into the building, and into what looked like the depths of Hell, actually a re-creation of an elaborate elevator maintenance shaft. You could hear the roar of the elevator ride as it raced up to the top of the tower with its riders. As it came plummeting down, the screams of the people sounded worse than the roar of the elevator car.

This was a terrible idea. My son was going to die. I had to get him out of the line. And that's when we were shoved onto the ride and buckled in.

Well, you can't win 'em all.

Right away, the elevator blasted off into the sky, squeezing my stomach into my toes. My son's smile disappeared instantly. He wouldn't survive. I think he knew it, too. The elevator car came crashing down. I wondered if the Earth's ground had disappeared since we kept falling and falling. My son went mute. I swore we left him in the sky somewhere.

When the ride should've been over, we were bounced back up into the heavens, and then shot down into the ground again. It repeated the motion a number of times, as if to make sure we stayed dead.

When we got off the death trap, I checked all my son's vitals. Surprisingly, he was alive. I asked if he was OK.

He jumped up and down. Because that's what he does when he's excited.

That could've been really bad, I thought.

For the moment, until my wife could kill me for suggesting we go on such a ride, I was safe.

Then I asked the boy, "Now you wanna go on something even faster and even scarier?"

— *August 2008*

FAMILY NEWS IN BRIEF

HUNGRY HIPPO CHAMP GIVES UP BIG LEAD, NEW CHAMPS NAMED

Having captured the most marbles in the first five minutes of last night's final game in the Hungry Hungry Hippo finals, my wife, last week's Hungry Hungry Hippo champion of our house, gave up a big lead when her hippo regurgitated several marbles and my five-year-old son and I snatched them up with our hippos, winning the game and the series in a tie between the two of us over Mommy. "My husband and son had only two marbles," my wife said after the game. "I had the rest, except for one in the center ring. And then there was some sort of toy malfunction where my hippo's mouth got stuck open, and the marbles that I'd already captured just rolled out and back into play. It's not fair." Sources say life isn't fair. My son and I acknowledged that fact, and then we accepted the victory.

YOUNG INVENTOR UNVEILS THE ZAPPER 3000

Earlier this month, my five-year-old son showed off his Zapper 3000, a machine that grants your wishes. "If you say, 'Zapper, turn off the lights,' the Zapper 3000 will shut off the lights," my son said during a recent demonstration. He asked the machine to turn off the lights, and sure enough, they went off. "I watched my son run over to the switch and turn off the lights," said my wife in a statement following the demo, "but he told me he didn't move. So I guess the Zapper 3000 really made the lights turn off." While the invention hasn't been used for anything other than the on/ off of lights and fruit snack delivery from the kitchen pantry to the living room, The Zapper 3000 creator says the machine can do much more. The innovation is still being beta tested, so time will tell if it's a success or not.

Tickets to the Moon Now Available

Trips to the Moon are now being offered in my home. My five-year-old boy built the first passenger space ship and he's flying passengers to the Moon four times a day. Tickets aren't available at the usual travel outlets, but my son is offering first-come-first-serve plans at the couch. After purchasing tickets, take a seat on his bed, and then, with the touch of a few buttons on the boy's toy laptop computer in the cockpit of the ship, he'll have you on the Moon in no time. Thrill at the sight of romantic sunsets from the Moon's surface, and enjoy magnificent panoramic views of cratered terrain on Earth-lit nights. Those planning to visit the Moon should pack for extremely hot days and ridiculously cold nights, and, of course, for "no atmosphere" conditions.

I Always Lose

I NEVER WIN. I WONDER IF THAT'S THE WAY IT'LL always be.

I lose in sports, I lose in those dice and word games you play on your phone; I never pick the winners at Oscar time; I never place in contests, except for that one countywide poetry contest I won in second grade, but that doesn't really count because the teacher entered my poem unbeknownst to me.

Eight years ago when my son was born, I made a promise that I'd save him from my bad gaming luck. Since then I've kept true to that promise — I always put him on the team against me. And he always wins.

A year or two ago, I stopped competing altogether. I'd come to the conclusion that excessive losing would eventually do something to my ego… or lack thereof.

All was well until some friends of the family asked if we wanted to participate in a day of park games.

"Yeah, park games!" my son said.

I loved the excitement.

Hated the idea.

I came up with an alternative activity: "How about we walk the dogs?"

I could've said I was sick or busy searching for the meaning of life. I would've been done with the whole thing and further along in my quest to find out why we're here, but our friends called me "chicken" and "fraidy cat." I couldn't walk away after that. I was too entertained by their paltry attempts to get me to play their games.

"You know," my son said, "legends say you're most likely to win when you have nothing to lose."

I don't know where my eight-year-old comes up with this stuff. He had a point. Maybe I could win if I just didn't think about it, like with my poem in second grade. I didn't think about it ever competing, and it was a winning piece of work.

I helped pack up the games — horseshoes, bocce ball set, water balloons, the basketball. We had a carload of games and refreshments for the day, and I was ready not to think about competing.

The players were all very competitive. "We're gonna kill you." "How's it feel to be the next biggest loser?" "I always win at this game."

Have you ever tried to not think about something you're actively doing? It's like watching a good movie — you can't help but get invested in the characters, the conflicts. You want the underdog to win. After almost winning a few games, I wanted to win even more. Yet, in those near-victorious moments, I never got cocky. I didn't talk trash like the others did. When ahead, I'd say to my competitor, "Well, you've still won more games than I have."

They'd respond with, "You actually think you're gonna win this one, don't you?"

The more I heard this and the more I lost, the more difficult it was to *not* think about it. I wasn't just losing the games. I was losing my dignity and my self-esteem. I couldn't help but think about it.

Why did I do this dumb park-games thing? I thought. *I knew this would happen.*

The people who played on my teams said what I was thinking. They suggested I sit out.

On my way to the sidelines, my son said, "Legends say that poor sports never win," which was ridiculous, I told him, because I thought I did a pretty good job suppressing my poor-sport attitude.

"If it's so suppressed," my wife said, "then why did you throw that water gun into the street and run out and stomp on it until it looked like sand?"

"I thought there was a bee on it," I replied.

The spirit of the park games fell hard. Our friends were quiet, bummed, looking for a way to cut out early. This was my fault. I'd put a damper on the whole day. I'd ruined everyone's time at the park.

Sweet bliss! That'd teach them to taunt me when I lost. I felt victorious for the first time all day.

That's when my wife came over to talk to me. I was sure she was going to blame me for everyone's bad time. I was sure she was going to spoil my only victory of the day. I was right — she did.

At her request, I joined in the final game. I really didn't care if I won or lost. I just wanted to go home.

If you thought this was going to be a story about how I turned the world's longest losing streak into a winning one, then I apologize for misleading you. I lost again. Royally. And everyone was happy again. They really liked when I lost and they won.

In the end, my friends and family forgot about my bad attitude earlier in the day. They all thanked me for a great time. And I was off the hook.

I got lucky. I guess I always get lucky. I wonder if that's the way it'll always be.

—*July 2012*

My Son the Comedian

SOME FATHERS TEACH THEIR SONS HOW TO PLAY baseball, with big dreams that their boys will play in the major leagues. My four-year-old son doesn't want to play baseball. He says he wants to be funny, so last weekend, I decided I'd take him to a stand-up comedy club.

I logged onto MySpace.com and found perhaps one of the funniest comedians on the comedy circuit today, New Jersey's Bad Boy of Comedy, Mike Marino. I wrote him an email and told him my son wants to be a comedian, and I asked if he had any advice. (My son is, in fact, pretty darn funny, but he'd need to do his homework if he was going to compete with the talent currently out there.)

Within a day or two, Marino emailed me back and said he'd get us into one of his upcoming shows. There he'd introduce my boy to the world of comedy. My son was very excited.

The bar was packed when my son and I arrived. While waiting for Marino to go onstage, the two of us ordered some cocktails. I got a Roy Rogers and my son got a Shirley Temple.

Some fathers play catch with their sons. My son and I were sipping drinks, eagerly anticipating the show that night, and discussing the standup comedy club surroundings.

"That big man over by the door — the man the size and build of an M4 Sherman tank — he's called a bouncer," I told my son. I went into all the details of a bouncer's position, the same way some fathers might explain the position of a baseball catcher or pitcher, and I did the same with all the other positions in a comedy club, so that my son would know all the comedy fields players.

During the conversation, Marino found us and came over to our table to say hello before he went on stage. He told us about how he got into stand-up comedy, what it takes to become a comedian and how he used his comedy talent to get into the movie biz. Before Marino left our table, I got him to sign my son's toy microphone — the microphone I bought him to use for his comedy routines (in place of the catcher's mitt I would've bought him had he been interested in baseball).

The show finally started, but we had to sit through a few other comedians' acts before Marino was on. My son couldn't wait to see Marino perform, as I'd shown him a few of Marino's video clips on YouTube. My son was anxious to see him in person. My boy loves Marino's bit about an Italian from Jersey as president of the United States, ending the war by sending two guys from the neighborhood overseas to whack Osama bin Laden with a baseball bat.

And speaking of baseball, had my son been interested in the sport, the two of us would've been sleeping at 11:00 p.m. on a Saturday night, getting in a good night's rest before waking up early for a Sunday morning game. Instead, we were spending a boys' night out at the club talking about the delicate use of the "F" word in a comedy routine. I told my son that he couldn't use the word at all in his routines until he was old enough. I think he understood.

After the show, Marino came back to our table and talked about comic timing, how setups relate to punch lines, and so on. My son took it all in. I think he's got the stuff that comedians are made of. Marino agreed.

Yes, I'm the proud father of a four-year-old kid with a future in stand-up comedy. Last weekend, my son hosted his first open-mike routine at our house to a sold-out garage. All the neighbors were in attendance.

Afterward, everyone went to Lampost Pizza and celebrated my son's successful routine. (We had to share the place with a youth baseball team that won their first game.) And that's when I woke up, realizing it had all been a weird dream.

But was it? Shortly after waking up, I found a Mike Marino-autographed microphone in my son's bedroom.

That's a true story.

— April 2008

BITS FROM THE 'BURBS

SPACED OUT

My first-grade son is learning more in school than I remember learning at his age. Thanks to the California Distinguished School he attends, he knows all the continents on the planet, he produces art that's suitable for framing and he can do math I couldn't do in college. Before winter break, he and his classmates each had to do an oral presentation in front of the class where they were graded on eye contact, the use of visual aids and the memorization of four lines of dialogue. My son's gonna be smarter than me within the year, which is fine, but I worry he doesn't have a chance to be a kid, that academics are consuming his life. He assured me, however, that he gets plenty of time to play. A couple weeks ago, while at recess, he said, he and some friends put a man into space.

QUEUE PILEUP

A new study reveals that when waiting in line to go on a ride at a theme park, stepping on the heels of the people in front of you and practically spooning them doesn't make you get on any faster.

LOSERS

My son played soccer this season. Toward the end of one of the games where his team was losing 10–0, my boy confronted the other team's coach and said, "Your team is doomed."

Fun Is a "Drag"

WHEN I WAS A KID, I NEVER GOT TIRED OF PLAYING with my Matchbox and Hot Wheels cars. When my mom dragged me to the store, I always had at least two toy vehicles tucked in my pocket for a race down the cashier's two-lane countertop.

My five-year-old son is the same way with his Matchbox and Hot Wheels cars, and he loves when I play cars with him.

Sure, I still enjoy playing with toy cars, except I need a pit stop after my 300th ride through the toy car wash.

"Don't you wanna drive anymore?" my son asked me on one occasion after fake driving for several hours.

"How about we play with the Lincoln Logs?" I suggested.

That wasn't the response my boy anticipated, and his response to my response wasn't what I was anticipating.

"Do you wanna switch cars?" he asked as he swapped cars with me, and then continued playing cars.

We both knew who was boss. I responded accordingly, "OK, we can play this game for another two days straight."

As I entered my 1,922nd fake car wash, my proverbial wheels were spinning, trying to figure a way to add some kind of spark to the game, and it hit me. I suggested that we gather all the Matchbox and Hot Wheels cars, pair them up equally and race them using my boy's toy drag-race launcher.

Race by race, round by round, we'd narrow down the competition until we found a winner.

My son lit up like a set of Goodyears at a green light when he heard the idea. I was actually excited, too. Which car would finish Number One?

We set up the drag-race launcher near the entryway of our home, and launched the cars down the Pergo floors toward the front door. Our queue of cars in line to race went down the hallway and spilled into the back bedroom. My wife nearly tripped over the cars as she rushed down the hall to answer the phone, sending my boy and me into a panic. She almost ruined 30 minutes of work we put into pairing up the vehicles.

When the dust cleared, I announced each race with my "monster truck voice," the voice you hear in those commercials for off-road spectaculars. You know, "SUNDAY, SUNDAY, SUNDAY! WITNESS THREE- THREE- 300,000 CUBIC INCHES OF HY- HY- HYDROLIC TORQUE! LIVE AT THE L.A. COLISEUM! WATCH TRUCK- TRUCK- TRUCK-A-SAURUS REX EAT NINE MILLION POUNDS OF SOLID MACHINERY!"

My wife, who was on the phone, was completely annoyed that my volume went into the red. I apologized for being loud. After a brief pause, I suggested she go into the other room.

My son and I had fun predicting the winners of each race. Any car could win. We'd set the cars on the launching platform, hit the button, and off the cars went. I suppose the heavier cars and the cars with the smoothest rolling wheels were most likely to win. Sometimes, however, even the best-equipped vehicles would spin out and crash into the couch or the wall.

For a while, my son kept picking the losing contender.

"Dad, you keep winning," he whined. "Can you let me win?"

I told him the outcome of each race was out of my control.

He considered my response.

"*Please*, can you let me win the next race?" he begged.

After three rounds of racing and over 300 individual heats, my son actually got tired of playing cars. I succeeded in burning him out. The game was driving him crazy, and he wanted desperately to play something else.

I took out his Lincoln Logs, cleared an open play area in the living room, and let the log building begin. I saw that my son was happy again.

I jumped right back into two more intense rounds of drag racing until I found a winner. I was bummed my '55 Chevy wasn't the grand champion. I attribute the loss to carpet fuzz in the wheels.

— September 2008

Gnome Sweet Gnome

I HAD TO HAVE A GARDEN GNOME.

My wife asked why I had the sudden urge to decorate the garden, and why a gnome.

"I just saw the little guy at the store and thought he'd look great in our garden," I said. "The question is: How can you *not* have a gnome in the garden?"

"Don't you think a garden gnome is like having those big pink plastic flamingos in the yard?" my wife asked.

"Oh, I have a pair of those on back order," I said. (I'm so glad my wife and I think alike.)

I set up our new garden gnome near the front gate of our home so that the terracotta elf could greet people who walked down the path toward the front door. I named the gnome Lampy, a good gnome name. There he stood wearing a red pointy hat, pipe in his mouth, welcoming every single one of our guests to our home. My wife seemed pleased.

"You know," I said, "the Germans used to believe that if gnomes were proud of their garden surroundings, they'd come to life at night when nobody was around and help with some of the landscaping."

My wife didn't respond. I think she was admiring the gnome splendor in our yard. My five-year-old son, however, seemed frightened by ol' Lampy.

"Does he really come to life at night?" he asked.

"That's what Daddy said," my wife answered. She told me that maybe we shouldn't have anything roaming around the yard at night. It would, in fact, scare our boy.

I worried. I didn't want to scare my son.

"He doesn't *actually* come to life," I admitted. "That's just an old German myth. Besides, Lampy here is a happy gnome, like one of Santa's elves."

My son ate up the Santa's elf bit. He was no longer scared.

I think my wife was happy that we were able to keep the gnome.

"Don't you think Lampy kinda sticks out like a sore thumb?" she asked. "We don't have anything else like it in the garden."

She had a point.

I ran down to the store and bought a couple more gnomes.

As I set up Bimpni and Lumwinkle in the garden, I told my wife and son that having gnomes was like having pets.

"We now have a lot of responsibilities," I said, "because gnomes require lots of attention and care."

"I don't know if we're really a good family for that kind of responsibility," my wife replied. "Since it's so much work, maybe we should take them back."

"No, no, it's OK," I told her. "I'll take on the responsibility. It'll be tough, but I think I speak for us all when I say it'll be worth it."

My wife fell silent again.

"Aren't you worried that someone will come along and steal the gnomes?" she asked. "God forbid we come outside to find them missing."

She reminded me of a game called "gnoming," where juveniles kidnap a homeowner's gnomes and send them on trips around the world, positioning them in front of various landmarks for photographs that later show up in the homeowner's mailbox.

I was stumped. I didn't want anyone stealing our gnomes, and I didn't know how to combat that kind of criminal behavior. I told my wife not to worry, that I'd sleep on it.

The next morning, last Sunday morning, I woke and went outside to check on our little gnome village. The gnomes were gone! I was outraged. My son said he wondered if they came to life and ran away. My wife took it the hardest. She put on quite the show.

"Oh, that's so terrible," she said. "And I loved them so much." She was clearly upset.

I bought another family of gnomes to cheer her up. My wife was surprised. I told her that that's what husbands are for.

She eventually came clean and said she never liked the gnomes. I was sad to hear the cold truth. To make her happy, I returned the gnomes to the store. Yes, my wife was happy.

Yet I wonder: What was so bad about my garden that made our first batch of gnomes run away?

— October 2008

MORE FAMILY NEWS IN BRIEF

ROCK CONCERT IS TONIGHT

Singer/songwriter/guitar player/harmonica player Little Picarella comes to my living room tonight as part of his Play, Play and Keep on Playing tour. Fans can expect to hear my five-year-old boy's hits such as "I Love Fruit Snacks," "I Love Candy" and "I Love Mac 'n Cheese," along with many favorites like "I Love Cake," "I Love Soda" and "I Love Gummi Bears" (aka "Bearway to Heaven"). My Son's music is a mixture of electronic toy guitar sounds and harmonica (key of C) noise. Once the music starts this evening at five p.m., it won't stop. It usually just keeps on going and going and going…

HOUSE FURNISHED WITH BUTTON PANELS

Following a recent visit to the hospital to see a sick friend, my five-year-old son decided to turn our three-bedroom home into a medical center, complete with all the necessary "machine buttons." The boy installed buttons at the foot of our beds, buttons on the arms of the couches and chairs, buttons on the walls in the hall and buttons below every light switch. "He's taken pieces of paper from our printer and drawn button panels on each sheet," my wife said yesterday. "Then he's taped them on practically every surface in the house." Asked what the buttons are for, my son said, "They're for kids not to touch."

Son Falls Down Slide, Hurts Teeth

Earlier this month, my five-year-old son was preparing to race a friend down the slide at a local playground when he stumbled over the ledge and took a head dive down the sloping chute, injuring his two front teeth and his upper lip. He took the necessary precautions the following day at school. "I told all my friends not to squeeze my teeth because they hurt," he said. Apparently our schools are filled with renegade kids who are squeezing each other's teeth. Local law enforcers weren't available to comment on the teeth-squeezing epidemic in the area.

Donna Vita Corleone: the Godmother of the Park

As far back as I can remember, I never wanted to be a gangster.

Last weekend at the park, I watched a group of parents line up to kiss some woman's hand. Must've been out of respect.

This woman — she entered the park from a back entrance I didn't know existed. She knew everyone. Everyone knew her or wanted to know her. She arrived, and the place went wild.

My five-year-old son and I arrived and nobody could have cared less. That was fine, but this woman's two kids were given immediate access to the play equipment, when everyone else had to wait in line for a turn.

"Excuse me," I said to this woman. "We were waiting in line to go next."

Have you ever heard a park full of noisy kids and talkative parents go instantly silent? Let me tell you. All eyes looked at me as if it'd be for the last time.

"We haven't met," this woman said to me. "You can ask around about me. If you could just allow me this once to cut in front of you, I know how to return a favor."

I told this woman to go ahead, said my son and I would play on something else. She hugged me.

"How would your son like to ride that red scooter over there?" she asked, pointing to one of the scooters parked at the bike rack.

"No, thanks," I said, coming to understand that this woman must've been some sort of Mafia Don. I knew not to get involved.

She called over to some woman sitting on a park bench, a woman she called Terri "Ten Kids" who, I'm told, gave birth to ten kids. This woman said that my son was going to take a spin on Terri "Ten Kids"'s son's scooter. Terri "Ten Kids" said it was certainly OK, and before I could turn down the offer a second time, my son jumped on the scooter and rode off down the sidewalk.

"Don't go too far," I yelled.

"It's OK," this woman said. "Nobody's gonna hurt him here."

I could feel this woman staring me down, probably trying to figure out if I was a good fella.

"Are you from the neighborhood?" she asked me. "What street do you live on?"

Jeez, this woman was pushy. And nobody pushed me around. Nobody. Except for maybe my wife and, of course, people who are connected, so I told this woman that, yes, I was from the neighborhood. I gave her the name of the street I lived on. I gave her my whole address, my phone number and even my social security number out of fear she'd have me whacked if I seemed out of line.

"I better go after my son," I said nervously. "He's gone too far."

The woman grabbed a hold of me — stopped me dead in my tracks. She said she'd send a couple of kids to get my boy instead.

When her goons returned with my son, she gave him some fruit snacks from her goodie bag and asked if he wanted to take the red scooter home for a couple days. My boy flipped with excitement over the fruit snacks and the scooter offer — he didn't know what kind of danger he was in. I told the woman that we couldn't accept either offer.

Before I could give the fruit snacks back, my son had already dug into the bag. I took his hand to leave.

"But what about the scooter?" he asked.

As I led him away, I said, "Leave the scooter. Take the fruit snacks."

Everyone at the park fell silent again. I should've accepted the scooter offer, but I knew what would've happened if I did. I'd be *in*. And once you're *in*, there's no getting out. Understand?

Two moms at the perimeter of the park, with their right hands in their coat pockets, stopped me from leaving.

"She'd like you to join her at the picnic tables," one of the moms said.

I told the ladies I wouldn't go to the picnic tables. They couldn't believe my response, as if I'd refused Don Vito Corleone — in this case, Donna Vita Corleone.

"She's gonna be disappointed, but we'll tell Her what you said."

After the message was delivered, this woman — the Godmother of the park — collected her kids and stomped off. The parents at the park turned and headed toward me. I knew how this worked. They'd line up to kiss my hand, a sign that there was a transfer of power, power I didn't want.

Turns out, everyone came over to tell me I'd been a jerk and that I'd hurt a nice lady's feelings, someone who just wanted to be friends with me.

I guess I've been watching too many mob movies lately.

— *March 2009*

Coming Soon!

I'M SOMETIMES ACCUSED OF TRYING TO GIVE MY KID everything he wants.

I know that's a bad idea because as much as I want to make him happy, I don't want him growing up thinking life will treat him the same way. I want to give him the skills and preparation he needs for the real world.

So when my son, now eight years old, asked to make a movie like the kind we watch in the theater, I initially wanted to say *yes* to make him happy, but because I went to film school, made movies and worked in the film industry, I said *no*. None of it is magic. The real world of the movies is heartache, pain and mostly failure.

I considered what was best for the kid. Heartache, pain and failure would all come along soon enough. I figured it'd be better for him to deal with letdown at a young age than be blindsided by it when he's older and the stakes become higher.

My son and I immediately went into production on the movie, using the family video camera and the movie editing software on the family computer.

Right away the kid and the movie didn't get along. Making movies takes time, and my son can't sit through the blink of an eye. But soon after realizing the workload he was in for, he quickly regained focus and plodded forward.

My son wanted his movie to have car chases, explosions and big monsters like in the films we watched in the theater. I knew the toy cars we pushed through the camera frame and the generic computer-generated explosions we applied via the editing program and the Halloween masks we wore were no match for the millions of dollars spent on the blockbusters my kid wanted to imitate. I just knew he'd be let down in the end, and it was going to hurt. It was going to be good for him, though. Right?

As we reached the end of post-production, my son was extremely proud and happy with the work we were doing. He was having a great time, too.

I think every filmmaker experiences such disillusionment.

As we watched the first cut of the film, I could almost taste the heartache to come. Friends and family would especially suffer through the 20-minute opus. I wouldn't be able to deal with the pain my son would soon experience. I kept telling myself that my son's pain now was better than his pain later.

But the kid loved his movie. It was everything he hoped it would be… and more. And he wanted everyone else to take the ride.

I couldn't deny him the opportunity. I gathered family and friends while he set up a movie theater in his room. I made popcorn. He cleared off his bookshelf to make a snack stand. I lined up the people outside his door. He ushered them into his theater, which even had aisles and seat numbers.

Before the start of the picture, my son instructed everyone to "please silence your cell phones." He dimmed the lights and "rolled film."

Everyone was impressed with my kid's directorial debut and fed his ego respectively. As a result, the up-and-coming

Spielberg wanted to make DVDs so he could sell them to strangers on the street. "You know, like how some kids sell lemonade," he said.

I had to set him straight. He made a great little video for his age, doing the best he could with the resources at hand, but no one but family was really going to buy it. I couldn't say anything, though. I didn't want to be the bearer of bad news. The look on my face said it all.

"Daddy," my son said, "I know it's not like a movie in the store. Maybe people will just want to support a kid and his art."

I didn't have to protect my boy after all. He wasn't under any false illusions — ever. He knew exactly what he'd made and he simply wanted people to see it for what it was. I was so glad I didn't have to let him down.

After my sigh of relief, my little filmmaker asked how we could get his movie nominated for an Academy Award.

— *March 2012*

MORE BITS FROM THE 'BURBS

BIKE RIDE

My son just learned how to ride his bike. Grandpa and Grandma, who live in Northern California, were on the phone with him, congratulating him. Grandpa asked him,

"Can you ride your bike up here?" My son said, "Up where? I can't see where you're pointing."

FRIENDS

The guy couldn't even say it to my face. He talks behind my back. He just said it to my face! Can you believe the nerve?

EVOLUTION OF A ROLLER COASTER

I used to think roller coasters were horrifying — the train could fly off the track, the seat harness could break and I could fall out, the stilts holding the track a million feet in the air could collapse and send me to my death. Eventually I became a teenager — smarter than everyone else — and I saw people getting off alive. I knew roller coaster makers had safety codes, standards, constant tests. Years passed and I experienced enough life to realize accidents do happen. Shortcuts in the workplace occur hourly. Procrastination and the lack of communication are the differences between "The track is fine" and "There's a section of track missing at the bottom of the hill!" At age 33, riding roller coasters is horrifying all over again.

The Girl, the Date, the Dilemma

It'd been a year since my son, now eight years old, met The Girl. The Girl's a year younger. This was their first play date since their first meeting.

"Do you remember her?" I asked my son.

"Yeah, Daddy," he said in a show-offy tone. "Of course I remember her. Duh."

"You met her last year," I said. "At this park. Her dad and I went to school together in San Francisco."

"I already know all that, Daddy," my son said, annoyed that I was filling him in with details when he just told me he remembered her.

"Do you remember her name?" I asked.

"Yeah," he said. "Duh."

I waited for him to say her name. When it was clear he had no intention of responding, I said, "So, what's her name?"

My son blew me off, ran to the playground. The Girl followed.

"Evidently," I told my friend, "knowing each other's name isn't grounds for being friends in the kid world."

I called for my son.

"It's OK," my friend said, probably embarrassed to be a part of this scene.

"No," I said. "He remembers her name."

"It's OK if he doesn't."

"Yeah, but I asked him a question and he just blew me off. That's not OK."

I called for my son again, this time using that fatherly voice that meant business. He'd come to me if he heard *that* voice.

My son just kept playing. I called again. Because I couldn't back down now. Luckily my son came over — I had no alternative strategy to show I held the power.

"Yeah?" he asked, as if I was inconveniencing him by calling him over.

"I asked you a question and you just ran off. That's rude."

"What was the question again? I forgot."

"I asked if you remembered her name."

"It's really OK if he forgot," my friend said, trying to end this whole thing.

"Yeah, Daddy," my son said with pure teenager in his voice. "I have to do stuff." He turned and ran back to the playground, my friend's daughter in tow.

I could've let the whole thing end there, but there were principles at stake. My son had stepped over a line. I stepped over that line after him. My friend followed, not because he was supporting me, but because he'd look kind of awkward standing on the outskirts of the playground alone.

I took my kid by the hand and walked him to a nearby park bench, sat him down.

"I asked you a question twice and you ignored me. And then you were rude. That's rude."

"Sorry, Daddy," my son said, no longer putting on the tough-guy persona.

"You've been doing this a lot lately. You repeatedly misbehave around other people to try and show off or something, and then you just want it all to be OK afterward because you say you're sorry. It's good to say you're sorry, but you have to start thinking before you act. Then you won't have to say sorry."

"OK, Daddy, I'm sorry."

"Now what was that girl's name?" I asked. "Do you remember it?"

"No," he said.

"Then why'd you lie and say you did?"

"I don't know. I'm sorry."

"You're not gonna get in trouble for forgetting someone's name," I said. I looked at my kid. He seemed to feel awful about the whole matter, so I dropped it. "OK," I said. "You can go play."

My son rejoined The Girl at the playground. I rejoined my friend. We stood there, quiet for some time, watching our kids play. I finally said, "He was embarrassed that he forgot your daughter's name. Silly, isn't it?"

Then I asked, "What's her name again?"

—July 2011

Summer Planners

To my wife and eight-year-old son, summer has endless possibilities. They want to *do* something. They want to do *everything*.

About a week ago, we received the city's "summer guide to mind-blowing fun" in the mail. Not only did this guide give my wife and kid *some* ideas for the summer, it gave them even *more* ideas.

"We don't have money for all these ideas," I said. "And I don't get that many days off work."

My wife informed me that her plans weren't set in stone. They were just ideas.

Needless to say, I couldn't control what my wife and kid were going to do or devise for the summer while I was at work. When I got home, I'd have to go along with whatever they threw at me.

For example, they planned my first day off—museum trips, playtime at the beach, a visit to a water-slide park and fancy restaurant outings. When I asked how we could afford to do all that stuff, even if we could fit it all in 24 hours and still get in a night's sleep, I became the bad guy.

"Guess who's being a sour sport?" my son said.

My wife told the kid that I wasn't being a sour sport. I was only looking out for the financial interests of our family. Thank goodness my wife understood where I was coming from.

"How about a trip to Hawaii?" she suggested instead. "We'll only go for a few days."

So when I said we couldn't afford museum trips, playtime at the beach, a visit to a water-slide park and fancy restaurant outings, Hawaii is her next idea?

While I was at work the next day, my wife put together a Hawaiian package, complete with car service to and from airports, air travel plans, hotel and dining arrangements and activity and event schedules.

I suggested instead one simple, inexpensive trip to the Grand Canyon for the summer.

"You don't have to pay to look into the canyon," I said, "and we can rent an RV, which doubles as transportation and sleeping arrangements."

"I can't sleep in an RV," my wife replied. "I'm a girl. I need comfort, showers … amenities." She told me an RV would go against everything I stood for — it costs money.

"Guess who's *really* being expensive?" my son chimed in.

"Hawaii isn't expensive?" I asked.

"The trip isn't set in stone," my wife responded. "It's just an idea — something to think about."

What was there to think about? Airplanes, hotels … lying on the beach with nothing to do but *not* think about work, bills or when I have to change the oil in the cars.

"Wow, you found some great deals," I said when I saw her Hawaiian research. "When do you want to go?"

But I soon saw that, as good of a deal as it was, we were still in no position to make the trip.

"I knew it," I said. "Why do you do this?" I bawled out my wife. "You come up with stuff we can't afford, we get excited about it and then we realize what we knew all along — we can't afford it."

I was pretty angry. It shocked my wife. My son noticed my wife's response to my behavior.

"Guess who's in trouble now?" he said. When he saw my response to his behavior, he answered his own question. "Me?" he said.

The next day I woke for work and moved through the house with very little communication between my family and me. When I got home, I apologized to them for getting so angry the night before. They apologized to me for getting my hopes up, though I couldn't let them take the blame.

Ah, why not? I thought. *Let them take the blame.*

I accepted their apology.

"I just wanted us to have a good summer," my wife confessed.

Lightning struck, which hit me as a surprise since brilliant ideas often come to my mind when it's too late to apply them.

We could do a camping trip, I suggested. The backyard could be the campground, the barbecue our campfire, the neighborhood pool a perfect lake, and the city pathways near our house could be our hiking trails. We could pitch the tent on our lawn. Best of all, it'd cost us nothing.

Everyone was on board. We swam, roasted marshmallows, took in the local floral and fauna and, before it got dark, we pitched a tent for sleeping.

"Where's your sleeping bag?" I asked my wife.

"Oh, I'm sleeping inside," she said. "I'm a girl. I need comfort, showers … air conditioning."

That night in the tent, as sweat poured off my body, I listened to the AC motor turn while it cooled my wife inside the house. I pretended the hard ground was as comfortable as my nice soft bed, all the while devising a surefire plan to get to Hawaii next year.

—*June 2012*

CHAPTER SEVEN

Finding Meaning

The American Nightmare

It's a Bird, It's a Plane...It's Suburb Man!

FAMILY MEN ARE ACTION HEROES. WE FACE A HORRI-
ble, treacherous nemesis, far worse than other superheroes
must face. We must stand up against the dreaded Domestic Gremlin, a creature not seen, but one that endangers our
precious domesticated lifestyle, causing kitchen appliances
to malfunction, allowing critters and other unsightly crea-
tures to enter wife- and kid-inhabited living quarters.

As a single young man, I saw my super powers as merely
average skills. As a husband and father, my super powers are,
well, SUPER!

If my wife sees a scary bug, one that will bite her head
off... Super Husband will destroy the pest and save the day!

If my son hears a scary noise outside his room while
sleeping, and he's afraid it's the killer cow that haunts his
dreams... Super Dad will go outside and defeat the "dangerous" quadruped!

Just call me Suburb Man. I use my super powers to fix
things throughout the house (inside and out).

I have super strength and can lift several bags of groceries,
all at the same time. I can open any screw-top jar, no matter
how tight the lid was fastened.

Even outside the home, my super powers come in handy.
At a restaurant the other night, for instance, our waitress

brought my wife the wrong drink. I used my super powers to draw the lady back to our table.

"My wife ordered a Diet Coke, not a Cherry Coke," I said.

Within seconds, my wife had the drink she ordered, compliments of Suburb Man.

I have a superhero costume. It's a really thick flannel shirt that nearly deflects bullets. I put on the "suit" any time I must carry out a super feat. At the end of the day, I hang my super suit on a rusty old spike driven into the wall of my very own "Bat Cave."

Yup, the garage (my Bat Cave) is where I keep all my wonderful toys like the ones Batman has in the movies. While Batman has things like a Bat wing, Bat smoke and Bat firepower, my superhero toys come in the form of screwdrivers, fly swatters and mousetraps.

That's right, I'm the real deal, a true action hero. I'm so super that maybe Hollywood will one day turn my story into a movie featuring action star Vin Diesel in the lead role. He's got about the right build to play me, no?

So all was well in the kingdom of suburbia when out of nowhere came a villain far worse than the Domestic Gremlin. At first sight, even I doubted my super powers as Suburb Man. This villain came in the form of a human of some sort, about five feet six, black hair, brown eyes, wearing a white coat that went down to her knees. She was armed with a piece of paper that said I needed to see a cardiologist.

Simply put: about a year ago, my doctor said she found some problems with my heart. A cardiologist later made me get a pacemaker.

My superhero powers were rendered useless. I don't know how I survived such a surgery, but in the last year of having this machine in my chest, I've developed a fear of doctors, never before having encountered such a hurtful individual for any reason other than to receive the harmless physical checkup necessary for me to play football as a kid.

The other day, at a routine checkup, my doctor suggested that I get my blood taken so the lab could check my cholesterol, even though, based on all the other million tests I did before having surgery, I looked as healthy as healthy can be.

"You don't have to do the test," my doctor said. "But it might be a good idea."

"Well, if I don't *have* to do the test," I replied, "then I won't."

She might as well have said, "I can punch you in the face if you want." Why would I want to endure something unpleasant? Needles are sharp. They poke through my skin, bust through my veins and suck up my blood. I'm fine without the intrusion.

My wife said I was being a big baby. She has no problem giving blood, and even my son has no problems with shots, she added, yet here I was, Suburb Man, acting like a coward.

The truth of the matter is that I never was a hero, at least not in my own eyes. I had no super powers, just average skills.

So there I stood, by choice, before my worst enemy, the doctor, who held a big, sharp needle. I laid down on a gurney, stuck out my arm and let this evil, evil being stick me with a needle and steal blood that was rightfully mine.

Finally, I really was an action hero, not for anyone else, but for myself.

Until next time!

— *May 2008*

I Suck!

IF YOU CAN'T SAY SOMETHING NICE, DON'T SAY IT *at all.*

We've all heard that saying a million times, yet people say the darnedest things.

I've hated my curly hair since I was a kid. It's nappy and grows all over the place. There's not much I can do with it. I try to keep it short, but it grows fast — and big.

When it's long, people like to remind me to cut it. "Your hair's getting nappy," they say. When I cut it, other people tell me to let it grow.

"Yo, gangsta," they say mockingly in bad imitation. "Where're yo Dickies pants and black Nike Cortez shoes to go along with that gangsta haircut?"

I can't win. How about I just become a different person?

The other day, a coworker asked me about the film school I spent so much money on and what it was like to be a failed director. Who says that kind of thing to your face? And how do you respond to that? Do you strike back? Or do you follow your conscience: *If you can't say something nice, don't say anything at all.*

I wasn't going to ignore this guy like I usually do when people say rude things, but I wasn't going to attack him either. Instead, I decided to turn his negative comment into a positive.

"OK," I said, "so I'm a failed movie director — true, but you have to fail early in life before you can succeed later. That's what I'm doing right now." My coworker was quick to shoot that down with a quote from author F. Scott Fitzgerald: "There are no second acts in American lives."

F. Scott Fitzgerald said it, which can only mean one thing: It must be true — I'm doomed to be a failure.

Thanks to an instant Internet search on my smart phone, I discovered that Raymond Chandler turned writer at age 45, Paul Gauguin was 43 when he became a painter, Martha Stewart was originally a caterer before becoming, much later in life, the superstar business magnate she is today, and Ray Croc was 52 years old, selling milkshake machines when he set out to build the McDonald's brand.

My coworker's not-so-nice comments actually led me to something inspiring. I wondered where I could get more painful criticisms.

I turned to my good friends. We met at a coffee shop for some sandwiches and hard truths. I got a healthy serving of both.

Right away my friends told me to get a haircut. Then came the juicy stuff: At 35 years old, I'm not making enough money, my house is a shack and I'm a terrible parent because I'm leaving my eight-year-old son an only child.

Well, my wife and I physically can't have another kid. That's beside the point. After another Internet search on my smart phone, I discovered that my wife and I are really good parents for having only one child. The world has shown us many incredible only children, including Franklin Roosevelt, Frank Sinatra, Elvis Presley, Cary Grant and John Lennon. Those are just a few recognizable names.

"How else do I suck?" I asked my friends as I wolfed down my BLT. With my smart phone nearby, I was hungry for more truth. My friends dished it out. Even my phone choked.

In the end, I came to the conclusion that I just suck. I suck at my job. I suck as a dad. I suck as a husband. Sure, I'm lucky to have a great wife and a great kid. I live in a great area. According to my friends, however, those things around me that are truly great are there to contrast with all the things within me that truly suck.

As the awareness of my suckiness sank in, I came to realize something cool. Without digging, I unearthed a positive aspect of sucking: If I suck at everything, then I don't have to be good at anything.

So I took advantage of my suckiness. When the bill for our sandwiches arrived, I informed my good friends that they'd have to pay my portion. "Sorry," I said. "I have no money. I know — I suck."

A few days later, my wife nagged me about my sucky driving. I pulled over and let her drive. My son said I wasn't being fair. I told him, "I suck, don't I? When we get home, you can clean your room."

That brings me to a recent piece of sucky writing I shoved in front of my wife for an honest opinion. I wrote the piece, so I knew it sucked. And I knew I couldn't fix it. Because I suck. I showed my wife anyway, perhaps as one last bit of evidence to confirm that I do, in fact, suck.

"It's really good," she said.

She didn't say she was confused. She didn't say it wasn't funny. She didn't even say I needed a haircut. She just said she really liked it.

Finally, someone had something good to say about me, something nice, which really could mean only one thing: My wife was lying.

— November 2011

FAMILY NEWS IN BRIEF

MAIL NOT DELIVERED, MAILBOX IS CAUSE

On Tuesday, the mailman failed to deliver mail to my home. According to my wife, both our neighbors received their mail that day. "Obviously, it wasn't a holiday or some other special day for the post office to take off," she said. "I started to worry that checks and important documents that I was expecting might've gone to someone else's house." Post office officials had no explanation for the lack of mail in the mailbox. The next day, my wife found a note in our box from the mailman explaining that he couldn't deliver the mail to our home the day prior due to the fact that the mailbox door wouldn't open. Inside our mailbox — the one our homeowners association replaced less than a year ago — was two days' worth of junk mail.

LAST CHANCE FOR LOW, LOW-COST EXTENDED WARRANTY

My wife and I were the lucky winners of an offer to buy a low, low-cost extended warranty for one of our vehicles. The guy on the phone said so. "This is a one-time offer that won't be offered again." My wife said thanks, but no thanks, and hung up. "Wouldn't you know it?" my wife later said. "The next week my husband and I were, again, the lucky winners of yet another offer to buy a low, low-cost extended warranty for the same vehicle, and this was the company's final offer. Again I said no." My wife and I have such good luck. Each week, for the last several months, we are the lucky winners of the same one-time final offer to buy a low, low-cost extended warranty for one of our vehicles.

Tv Broke, Conversation a Must

At 9:22 p.m. on Saturday, January third, during my five-year-old son's first slumber party with his friends at my house, the TV in the master bedroom stopped working. For the remainder of the evening, my wife and I were forced to hold steady and focused conversation. "At almost ten p.m. on a Saturday, after our five-year-old and his slumber buddies had already gone to sleep on the living room floor, what were my husband and I to do but talk quietly in our room?" my wife told sources. "We couldn't leave the house, we couldn't watch TV in the living room, and neither one of us was tired. Any slight noise we made, aside from talking very low, woke at least one of the kids. Yup, my husband and I talked — for two whole hours." Asked how I held up during the January third talk-a-thon, I answered, "Anything and everything I said was held against me."

Just Say Thanks

Thanksgiving is a day to give thanks.

So when my wife's aunt and uncle invited us to their home for Thanksgiving a second year in a row, we should've said thanks but no thanks. Instead, my wife agreed to go.

Then I felt guilty.

"But they had us over last year," I said. "We should be inviting them over this year."

I believe that if a friend treats you to coffee, you should treat him to coffee next time. I can't see abusing another person's giving nature. A gift must be returned.

"We're in no position to host Thanksgiving this year," my wife said. "And my aunt and uncle aren't like that. A return gift isn't necessary. Our thankfulness is plenty."

Maybe my wife was right. Maybe the gift doesn't have to be returned. Maybe saying thanks is enough.

As a result of that revelation, I spent the month of November saying thanks and not feeling in debt to anyone who gave me something or did something for me. If people performed such a kind gesture, I thanked them. That was it.

My mom, who writes thank-you letters for thank-you letters, thought I was nuts. Typically, we'd be spending Thanksgiving with her this year at her home in Northern California since we spent last year with my wife's family in Southern California—we alternate from year to year. But my mom made plans to be out of town this Thanksgiving, so we'll be in the southland for 2011.

"You're going over to her aunt and uncle's again?" my mom said. "Michael, you should be having *them* over this year. You have to return the gift."

"A return gift isn't necessary, Mom," I said with my new outlook on life. "Our thankfulness is plenty."

I went on behaving with that mentality.

Last month, when my wife and I celebrated our 11th wedding anniversary, a friend from work bought us a present. This month, that same friend celebrated his wedding anniversary. I felt no obligation to return the gift. I just congratulated him on five years. (I never thought outsiders should give gifts to those celebrating their anniversaries anyway.)

Last week, when I was running late for work one morning, my neighbor helped me out by taking my son to school. I thanked her, and I didn't feel obligated to give her son a ride to school the next morning when she was running late for work. I just waved to her as I drove away.

A dinner out, thanks to my sister-in-law, went unreturned. All compliments went unreturned, though I sincerely thanked anyone with nice words.

The same behavior applied to casual greetings. If someone said to me, "Hi, how are you?" I didn't feel obligated to say, "I'm well, how are you?" back. Not anymore. When anyone asked how I was, I'd say, "I'm well. Thanks." And I'd move on.

"Thanks." That was it. I felt no guilt to return the gift until I felt guilty for not feeling guilty about returning the gift. Worse, my wife was getting complaints from friends and family saying I was ungrateful.

"But I said thanks."

Everyone who had done something for me this month had cut me off. I was dead to them.

I thought maybe I could give return gifts to redeem myself, but either it was too late or I couldn't financially afford to return the gifts.

"I told you," my mom said when I called for advice. "You can't accept anything else."

That was it — I wouldn't accept anything else, but no one was offering anything else.

So I say here and now, thanks to all my friends and family for just being there. I don't need anything else. I'm thankful for what I have. I'm thankful for the people in my life, for my community, for the roof over my head, for the food on my table.

Wow, that's what Thanksgiving is really all about, isn't it? It's about giving thanks for what we already have.

Thanks.

Now who's gonna give the thanks back?

— *November 2011*

A Great Family Man

I'M A GREAT DAD TO MY FOUR-YEAR-OLD SON AND A great husband to my wife. I believe that because my mom told me so, and she wouldn't lie about something like that, not this close to Father's Day.

She added that I was a great family man like her father—my Grandpa Balsamo. This was a huge compliment. I felt touched. I felt honored. I felt like my mom was going to say, "Hah, just kidding!"

I've known since I was a young boy that my Grandpa Balsamo loved to play the saxophone and the clarinet, but I thought he did it strictly for fun. I later learned that at one time he made money as a musician and had hopes of playing music for a living.

Unfortunately, because it was such a tough profession during difficult economic times, my grandfather was more likely to go pro as a rock/paper/scissors player than to make a living as a musician. Marriage and family took his mind off his struggles. Eventually he was forced to take work as a machinist if he was going to support his family.

Since my grandpa's death, I've often wondered if he was disappointed that his music career never took off. I wonder if he regretted taking work as a machinist. I'd like to know his true feelings on that.

I asked my mom what she thought, and she said my grandpa was always happy. She said she'd send me a video interview that my aunt had conducted with him for a college course. My mom said I might find what I was looking for there.

While I waited for the package to arrive in the mail, I dug up a picture of my grandpa when he was about my age. He was sitting at a workbench in his garage repairing an instrument, a job he did during the day to make extra money while he played music at night. Like always, my grandpa was grinning in the photograph, but I wondered, was his smile true or just for the camera? Was he worried that repairing instruments was earning him more money than playing instruments?

My grandpa's skill with his hands would soon allow him a career outside the music business, an opportunity that would provide the money he needed to support his family. Did he know such a fate was ahead? Sitting there repairing that instrument in the photograph, one leg relaxed over the other, was my grandfather settling into a life unfulfilled, the reality of playing music professionally slowly slipping away?

I have dreams, just like my grandpa had, and I've had to put them on hold at times to make a living to support my family. I know the feeling of defeat, and I know the feeling of fear that my dreams are slipping away. But I always try to convince myself that it's only a temporary defeat and not permanent. I tell myself that even Superman couldn't support himself rescuing people — he had to become Clark Kent and work a day job at the *Daily Planet* in order to make ends meet. I try to believe that one day my dreams will become a reality if I just keep trying.

My mom's video showed up in the mail after a couple of days. I watched my grandpa's interview with great enthusiasm, examining every frame carefully, looking for clues to this man's passions in life, his successes and his failures, and for telltale signs as to whether he made the choice to abandon his dreams or if he had no choice in the matter.

I learned that my grandpa's dad, my great-grandfather, died before my grandpa was in his teens. My Great-grandmother Balsamo had to raise eight children alone.

In the interview, my grandpa said that, despite what happened with his dad, his was a very happy family, and that he was a happy kid. He did lots of fun things like working a paper route, attending school and shining shoes at a barbershop. Fun?

Each family member, young and old, my grandpa said, had to pitch in around the house and work so that the fatherless family could survive. Regardless of the number of chores they did, everyone was happy because they had each other.

Later in life, my grandfather and my grandmother would raise five girls. Everyone was so content, according to all. My mom tells me that my grandpa always put his family first — before work, before music, before everything. My mom has told countless stories to prove this, which is why her telling me I was a great dad like hers so deeply moved me.

In spite of how I felt, I couldn't help but wonder if I was heading down the same path that my grandpa traveled, for better or for worse. I wondered if my dreams would ever come true.

Before my grandpa died almost five years ago, I visited him in the hospital. He asked about my personal dreams and if I was still pursuing them. Yes, I said, I was still working my way toward my goals.

He smiled, as if he knew the challenges and almost as if he knew my fate, and then he asked me about my family — my wife and newborn son. I said we were all very happy. He smiled again. That was the last I saw of my grandpa alive.

About six months ago, I learned about a really bright girl who graduated from high school with outstanding grades and honors. She was offered $185,000 in scholarships for college — an unbelievable opportunity. She turned it down.

I found out she grew up in a fatherless home with no siblings. For many years, she lived on the street. Instead of accepting the scholarships and an education, this girl got married to someone who really couldn't support her, and the two of them started a family. It seems that building a family was more important than anything else to this girl.

Still, so many people around her, including myself, couldn't believe she turned down so much money and an education, which would've made her life so much better.

I wonder if my grandpa were in the girl's place today, which way would he go? If I were in the girl's place today, which way would I go? Which way would you go?

—June 2008

BITS FROM THE 'BURBS

THE TRUTH

I never lie. That's a lie, isn't it?

FREE COUCH

My six-year-old son and I were on a walk to the park when we came across a couch someone had placed in front of their house at curbside, a sign on the couch indicating it was free for the taking. I stopped my son before he could sit down — the couch was filthy. Nobody in his or her right mind would accept this free gift, let alone put it in their home as an actual piece of furniture. The couch sat on the street for about a week. Even the "Free" sign survived all seven days. One morning, while driving by, I noticed someone replaced the "Free" sign with a sign that read "$50." Someone stole the couch within the hour.

NICE TO MEET YOU

I might seem happy, but I'm not. Sometimes when I'm not happy, I am. I'm really multilayered. That said, I'm easy to figure out.

A CHANGED MAN

I know... I'm not normal. I haven't been myself since I was two.

I Want a Reason

IT WAS JUST A ROUTINE CHECKUP.

I'd had a pacemaker in my chest for a little more than a year at the time, due to a slow heart rate and frequent blackouts. While the technician assessed me and my pacemaker, I noticed her eyes growing bigger. Without taking a breath, she suggested there might be a problem with my heart.

She asked me to lie down, told me to calm down, relax… then she shot out of the room to get a doctor.

I checked my watch. I was late for another engagement. When the technician finally returned without the doctor, I stood up and asked if this was really necessary — I was expected at Al Pacino's AFI Life Achievement Award ceremony in Hollywood.

"We might have to check you into the ER," the technician told me.

"You don't understand," I replied. "I *have* to go to this Pacino thing. My mother-in-law got these tickets, and she's waiting for me."

My always punctual, very disciplined mother-in-law had been gifted two tickets to the event by a business friend, and had invited me to go with her because she knew how much I loved movies.

Luckily for my insurance company, my heart didn't cut out that day, and my mother-in-law and I made it to the event on time.

Things don't always work out so well. I think it's safe to say that life, in general, doesn't work out so nicely, not even for those of us who get to see Al Pacino in person.

My mother-in-law passed recently, unexpectedly. I'd like to believe there's a good reason for it.

Maybe she'd already accomplished what she needed to accomplish in life, so her work here was finished. She started out in a tiny house in East L.A., next door to a family of gypsies. From there she established a successful banking career and helped raise a happy family; happy despite (or maybe because of) her strict business-like regimen, which included grocery store lists organized by the aisle and frequent yodels for her husband from the second-story landing of their home. "RRRRROSSSSSS!" she'd lovingly call on a regular basis, summoning his immediate assistance.

My mother-in-law was a daughter, a sister, a wife, a mother, a grandmother, a banker, an expert witness, a teacher, a consultant... a fellow *Godfather* movie lover. Most recently she served as the chief of staff for the western director of the FDIC and, although she was diagnosed with lung cancer earlier this year, she prepared for the end of that job and freshened up her resume to apply for new positions. She wouldn't give up easily. She couldn't. She knew tomorrow the sun would rise and so would the family she loved. She had to keep on going. She had more to do.

No, I don't think my mother-in-law felt she'd accomplished what she needed to accomplish. I don't think that explains her premature death.

Maybe she passed because God needed her in Heaven to watch over her family from an even loftier perch than her earthly one. She did like being high up in the ranks, and the higher-ups always liked her.

Here's how I imagine that going: She gets to the pearly gates and St. Peter checks out her resume, gives her a heck of an interview. His job depends upon on whom he lets in and whom he sends away, so understandably he's nervous. *What if,* he wonders, *God likes the throw pillows right where they are?* And can you imagine God, relaxing while watching over the world, suddenly hearing from some second-story cloud: "GAWWWWWWWD!" That'd spell the end of St. Peter's career. So St. Peter asks my mother-in-law her intentions.

"All I plan to do if I get in," she responds, "is make sure my family stays safe." So she's up there right now, watching carefully over us all.

That sounds like a nice scenario. I'd like to believe that's the reason behind my mother-in-law's untimely death; that she left so she could keep better watch over us all. I think the whole family would like to believe that's the reason, and yet I can't quite buy it. I'm certain she could have kept all of us safe and in line just fine from down here.

No, I think the real truth lies in a passage I came across while reading the Bible. I haven't read the Bible much, but I picked it up and thumbed through the book of Ecclesiastes, where it says, "There is a righteous man who perishes in his righteousness, and there is a wicked man who prolongs his life in his evildoing." In other words, any of us may go at any time, and there's no reason for why or when.

The book also offers this: "There is nothing better for people than to be happy and to do good while they live, that each of them may eat and drink, and find satisfaction in all their toil."

My mother-in-law did just that. She loved her work. She loved her family. She loved her days on Earth, and she wanted the same for others. She *really* did, which is why, I think, she waited a few extra days to make her final exit last week — to make sure her loved ones would be happy and doing some good in life.

My father-in-law will tell you — his wife always got what she wanted. She wouldn't just give up. She couldn't. Yup, when she left, she left on her own terms, satisfied, knowing that tomorrow the sun will rise.

And so will we.

— September 2011

Grand Poobah

I CAN NEVER SAY NO.

I was helping my wife glue paper rainbow cutouts onto a page in one of her scrapbooks when my father-in-law called and asked me to check my email. I couldn't say *no*.

I don't like confrontation and I try to stay in everyone's good graces, so even though I feared that my father-in-law's email might contain painful requests like, "Can you give my daughter a better lifestyle" or "Please give her back," I went to my computer and opened my mail.

Dear Mike, the letter began. *When you married my daughter in 2000, I thought it best we combine forces to provide the highest level of male support we could achieve. Thus, the Misunderstood Husband's Club and Rowing Society was born.*

I was voted the esteemed Grand Poobah, and you, thankfully, assumed whatever other roles were left. It is with great sadness, then, that I resign my position to you, as I feel I am no longer qualified to carry on my leadership.

I stopped reading the letter right there. I couldn't fill my father-in-law's shoes. I didn't have the skill, the experience or the time. How could I lead? How could I say *no*?

As I continued reading the email, I tried imagining myself as the new head of the Misunderstood Husband's Club and Rowing Society.

Since the beginning, our club flourished and provided support for both of us when dealing with our wives, my daughter and other assorted female friends and relations. Oftentimes, when faced with mysterious female logic, the only thing that saved the day was discussing the problem during our monthly meetings at the R.E. Pool Memorial Shelter for Downtrodden Husbands (an old Dew Drop Inn).

I recalled my father-in-law's unequivocal headship at those meetings and his firm ability to reel in an emotional speaker. I was then reminded of the calm and cool he exuded during the incident he described next in his email.

The well-known Junk Food Jaunt best exemplifies our wives' misunderstanding of our innocent actions. If you recall, we dropped our wives off at Zumba class for their weekly exercise, and instead of waiting out front as promised, we shuttled across the parking lot to the nearby 7-Eleven for a sweet snack or two.

A late class member noticed us consuming the tasty treats, and upon entering the building, she ratted us out. The dirty looks we received once the Zumba class let out proved the lady sung like a bird. There was no use trying to deny our guilt—the evidence was all over our hands and faces.

Instead of receiving affirmation for taking our wives to Zumba, we were chastised for consuming a perfectly legal item.

I distinctly remember the skirmish, and I remember speaking my mind openly at one of our meetings later in the week. Perhaps I spoke a little too openly. However, my father-in-law, the Grand Poobah, calmed me down, and reminded me of the vow I took when I said *I do*— "You must," he said, "above all, serve, protect, obey, and say, *Yes, dear.*"

I could never settle a shaken husband of the club that quickly or that effectively. In other words, I could never be Grand Poobah. I could never accept my father-in-law's resignation. He would have to continue his reign.

I finished reading his email, which had more group nostalgia and farewell babble. Afterward, I consulted my wife on the matter.

"Why me?" I asked her. "I can't be leader. But I can't say *no.*"

"Why can't you say *no?*" she asked.

Then it occurred to me — *Yeah, why can't I say no?*

I used to say *no* all the time.

When I was a kid, I'd say *no* to strangers if they offered candy or I'd say *no* to friends with dumb suggestions like, "Hey, you should roll that tire down the street into oncoming traffic." At some point during my "growing up," I became a pushover.

I wouldn't be easily swayed any longer. I picked up the phone, called my father-in-law, and began talking about random subjects until I could find a transition point to tell him *no.*

Before there was such an opportunity, he said something that had previously slipped my mind.

"Had it not been for the untimely death of my wife (back in August), I would've continued my leadership of the club…"

Thus, for the first time in years, I told someone *no*. My father-in-law said, "You don't have to take over as Grand Poobah if you don't want to."

I said, "No, I'll be happy to take over."

My father-in-law, according to his email, will remain a mentor to the group.

— May 2012

MORE FAMILY NEWS IN BRIEF

TALKER TALKED AND TALKED

My wife and I attracted a talker at a neighborhood eatery earlier this month, and we couldn't break away. Individually and as a couple, we draw in talkers. "It's like there's a sign on my head that says, 'Talk to me, and don't let me get in a single word,'" said my wife. The recent talker, who talked and talked and talked, started talking about the weather after my wife and I said, "Good afternoon," and then he transitioned into talk about the Florida Gators being the first football team to test Gatorade. We also learned that the Greek word "gymnasium" means "to exercise naked." Eventually, the talker made a crucial mistake — he stopped talking to take a breath. We told him we had to go.

GIRL LATE FOR SCHOOL

A local kindergartener was allegedly late for school earlier this month. The student's spokesperson, Mom, said her daughter's tardiness was excused. "I sent her with a note," Mom said. Since the incident, half the class has been asking if they could be tardy for class as well. "Which day can I be late for school?" asked my own kindergartener during what is now being dubbed the "I Also Wanna Be Late For School Crisis." School authorities said classroom attendance and punctuality are the necessary ingredients for success in any endeavor, school included, and they suggested that kids not be late or absent if they can help it. "However," an anonymous school official said, "we will excuse a student if he or she has a note."

ELECTION HEATS UP

As my son's first day of kindergarten nears, nobody can clearly say who will win dibs on that first goodbye kiss. My wife's campaign for the kiss is going strong with support from as far as her uncle in South Carolina. My support doesn't leave the state, but it might be enough to garner that first smooch on Wednesday, August 13th. "I just want to kiss Mommy and Daddy," said my son in a statement earlier this week. Conservatives feel that my wife's lips are what my son really needs first for that all-important goodbye because, as the mother, sources said, she gave birth to the child. Liberals, on the other hand, said that it's time for a change and that, in this democratic nation, either parent should have a chance at the first kiss. Tonight will begin a series of debates between the two candidates. I'm thinking I have a chance.

Nothing for Mom

A FEW DAYS BEFORE MOTHER'S DAY LAST YEAR, MY mom called and told me not to buy her anything. She said she didn't need anything, that she wanted my sister, my brother and me to save our money.

How could I not get my mom something for Mother's Day?

"You don't have to give me something to show your appreciation," my mom told me. "You prove your appreciation every day."

How kind of her.

But how kind would I be if I didn't get my own mother something for Mother's Day? I told my wife about my mom's ridiculous request.

"You have to get her something," my wife said. "You don't want her to be sad, not on Mother's Day."

"But I *can't* get her something," I responded. "I don't want her to be mad, not on Mother's Day."

I did the logical thing — I flipped a coin. Heads — I'd send a gift. Tails — I wouldn't send a gift. Tails it was. I sent a gift anyway.

When my sister called to stress the importance of not buying Mom something, it was too late. My order had already shipped.

"She's gonna freak," my sister told me. "You have to cancel the order."

"OK," I said. "I'll call the company right now."

Instead I talked to other family members about what I'd done.

"I bought my mom this for Mother's Day," I said, showing a picture of the gift. Everyone loved it and said my mom would love it, too. "But," I added, "she told me not to buy her anything this year."

"You bought her something anyway," a relative scolded me. "That's awful, Michael."

I tried to cancel the order. The lady on the phone was one of the most helpful customer service individuals I've ever dealt with.

There was nothing she could do — typical customer service.

My brother called, asked if I was sending Mom a gift. He said he wasn't. I told him I wasn't either. My sister called to see if I cancelled my order. I said I cancelled it. My mom called to make sure I didn't buy her a gift. I said, "Of course I didn't; I wouldn't go against your wishes, not on Mother's Day."

I was doomed.

Then I found the solution to my problem. I'd just say I knew someone at this store who owed me a favor who got me the gift and the shipping for free.

My sister thought it was a good save.

"But," I said to her, "will you feel bad that I got Mom something and you didn't?"

My sister assured me that she wouldn't feel bad. That was a load off my mind.

"But Mom will feel bad that you're the only one of her kids to get her a gift," she said. "You know Mom, she'll feel bad for those of us who didn't get her something."

I told my sister I'd fix the problem. I'd drive from Southern California to Northern California, where my mom lives, and grab the package off her doorstep before she got home on Saturday.

Five hours later, when I got to my mom's house, I thought about how ridiculous this all was — my mom didn't want us kids to spend money, but here I spent gas money on a ten-hour round-trip to pick up a gift I'd paid for and couldn't return. As I walked up the driveway, I considered leaving the gift, turning around and going home. Better yet, I'd surprise my mom with the gift and a visit.

At the door, I saw my gift. And I saw two others — one from my brother and one from my sister. Those rascals.

My mom loved all the presents, and couldn't stop talking about how appreciated she felt. She was not mad at all. She was happy. I'd go as far as to say that last Mother's Day was one of my mom's best. We kids did the right thing.

My mom just called. She told me not to get her anything for Mother's Day this year, that she doesn't need anything. She wants us kids to save our money.

And so, to the Internet stores I go.

— May 2011

WINNING!

I'M NOT ONE OF THOSE COMPETITIVE PARENTS WHOSE kid has to win at everything. I'm the parent who just doesn't want his kid to lose.

So when my nine-year-old boy was playing handball with friends and losing royally, I wanted to step in and save him, call "cheating" on the other side and help him play better by playing for him, but I couldn't intervene.

Instead, I ended the handball session, telling my son we had to run a family errand, and I took him to the store and bought him a handball.

At home, we worked on his handball game. I set up a rigorous practice schedule — a two-hour session, six days a week for three straight months. Next time he played, he wouldn't suffer a loss.

Problem: After the first day of practice, we never got around to practicing again.

Last weekend, some of my son's friends asked if he wanted to play basketball. My kid begged to play. I told him we had family errands to run.

My son was all frowns. After his friends left for the park, he asked what was so important that we had to do. I explained that we didn't have to do anything and that I just made up an excuse to spare him from humiliation.

"Why did you do that?" he asked.

"Son, are you even good at basketball?"

"Yeah. I play at school all the time. And I really wanted to play with my friends."

He was hurt.

We caught up with his friends at the park just in time to play. The kids picked teams and decided that the first team to reach 20 points would win. I chomped on my nails as the players took to the court. I thought about turning away so I wouldn't have to see my son lose, but I couldn't help it. I watched.

He was actually pretty good. He even sank a jaw-dropping three-pointer. I didn't think he could throw the ball that far, let alone make the shot. He continued to make more amazing shots. It was Ripley's Believe It or Not right before my very eyes. I called for a time-out, pulled my son aside.

"What's going on, why are you so good?" I asked, as if he was pulling some trick.

"I play at school every day, Daddy," he answered.

I told him to keep it up. He was great. He even played great defense — blocking shots, grabbing rebounds. My son's team was destroying the competition.

Then, a few minutes later, the competition struck back. A 13–4 lead became a meager 13–12 lead. My son was missing easy shots. He practically dusted off the ball, scrubbed it clean and handed it to the defenders.

The other team took the lead, 14–13, and talked some serious trash. They stole the ball from my son, laughed in his face. One player pushed my kid to the ground. Ouch! That really hurt. The other team ran off with the ball and scored the winning shot.

My son had scraped his knee and was in serious pain. He tried to look tough for his friends, and walked it off. I so wanted to step in, but I didn't want to embarrass him more by coddling him. At least the game was over and we could go home before any more damage occurred.

We weren't that lucky. The kids wanted to play hide-and-seek. I didn't get a chance to say *no*. They chose my son to be it, and he went along with them, limping around the park while everyone hid from him.

It continued to get worse. We somehow ended up back at our house for video games. We were short one controller. The kids decided that my son would have to sit out and my son just let it happen. I couldn't let him suffer any longer. I was going to intervene this time, whether right or wrong.

Instead, my wife ended the misery, telling the kids it was time for them to go, that we had family errands to run.

Wow, those kids must've thought, *that family sure runs a lot of family errands.*

I thanked my wife for rescuing our child, for saving him from more losing, more pain.

"I didn't do it for him," she said to me. "You looked like a wreck over there. I couldn't take it."

"Daddy, I'm OK," my son added. "I don't care if I lose. I let them win because they get mad when they don't. I also don't care about not playing video games. I can play whenever I want."

He let me in on another secret — he'd missed those shots on purpose and was happy to be *it* during hide-and-seek so someone else wouldn't have to do it. I was proud to have such a caring kid.

We played a video game together. He killed me. Evidently, he was through with charity work.

— *March 2013*

MORE BITS FROM THE 'BURBS

OUCH

"Hurt people hurt people." I thought I made that up. Then someone told me it was from a movie. That hurt.

OUCH PART TWO

Sticks and stones may break your bones, but names will kill ya every time.

HONEST

I like people who let me know where I stand... as long as they like where I'm standing. Otherwise I hate those pompous jerks.

THAT'S HEAVY

I found a new "scale" app in the app store. My phone snapped into pieces before I could read my weight.

DINNER

Salsa and chips is no meal. Got home from work. I'm tired, hungry. Nothing easy to make. Checked the cupboards. Checked the fridge. Salsa and chips it is.

LET'S GO!

I hurry now so I won't have to hurry later. Ah, it's later. I'm in a new hurry.

ANY MONEY?

Take out the "r" in "free" and look what you got. Always.

Eye Love You

LIVING WITH BOYS WILL DRIVE YOU CRAZY. MY WIFE knows — she's got our nine-year-old son, our three-year-old male beagle and, last but certainly not least, me.

We don't try to make her crazy.

"You're all so loud," she said one day. "Between the sound effects and the made-up words to songs and the howling and the barking. That doesn't even include the noise from the dog."

"I thought you were a huge fan of my song work," I said.

"You know it drives me nuts," she responded.

"But I love you," I told her.

"And that's what I hate most," she said. "You never take responsibility."

OK, so I could see we were driving her slightly mad. I decided to give her a break. I told her I'd take the kid to his eye exam that afternoon so she could stay home for some peace and quiet.

"Is that bad that I'm not going, too?" she asked.

"It's just an eye exam," I said. "It's really no big deal."

It was a big deal to our son. He didn't want to go. He feared eye appointments.

Great, now I'd have to deal with this all by myself. I had to be persuasive with the kid, make him feel comfortable, convince him that an eye exam is really no big deal.

"Get in the car," I said. "We're going."

At first glance, the eye exam machines looked like something out of the *Terminator* movies, which didn't make my son feel any better about what the doctor was going to do to him.

"It'll be OK," I said. "It's really no big deal."

The eye doctor put my son at ease — initially, anyway.

A few minutes into it, the kid got silly. When the doctor asked him to look left, right, up and then down, my son became a comedy act.

"I roll my eyes at my parents all year long just to practice for this," he joked.

The doctor did that puff-of-air test in the eye.

"Did you spit on me?" my son asked with a giggle.

While waiting for the test results, the doctor showed us a computer-generated eyeball.

"Is this thing like Google Earth?" my son asked as the doctor explored deeper into the eyeball like he was looking for a destination on our planet. My son's awesome humor kept coming.

At the end of the checkup, we learned that my son's eyes were in great health. That was that.

"See," I said when we got in the car to go home. "It's really no big deal. Easy."

At home, my wife asked, "When was the last time *you* had your eyes checked?"

"Me?" I responded. "I already went. I'm good."

"You may be good, but *when* did you go?"

"I went only four years ago. My eyes feel fine. It's really no big deal."

"Again," she said, "not taking responsibility, like usual."

"But I love you," I said.

I knew what was coming next — she'd claim I was setting a bad example for our son, and my son would turn my "It's really no big deal" words against me to get me to go to the stupid eye doctor.

"They're *your* eyes," my wife said. "Do what you want."

"At least *my* eyes are perfect," my son added.

What was this? They couldn't care less about my health.

I called the eye doctor for an appointment. He'd care about me.

He didn't have any openings — not for a while, anyway. I set a date. My wife and kid were happy for me. I was actually happy, too.

"When's the appointment?" my wife asked.

"June," I said.

"That's four months away!"

"Not *this* June," I told her. "The June after."

"June of 2014!"

"But I love you," I said.

I wasn't lying.

—January 2013

The Earth Shakes, the Seas Rise

MY SEVEN-YEAR-OLD SON HAS BEEN IN LOTS OF TROUble lately. Discipline doesn't help.

I dropped a 30-pound box of garage junk from a high shelf into my eyeball. There's a big red blotch on my eye that feels like a sharp wooden splinter.

Oh, and a close relative just got diagnosed with cancer. It's stage three.

To make matters worse, I injured my back and I can barely stand. The pain medication has made me extremely anxious, hyper and insensitive.

Someone tried to "cheer me up" with, "Stop whining, it could be worse."

The aftereffects of my pain medication kicked in and I said insensitively, "Oh, so because it's not worse, because my family isn't living on the street, because we still have our limbs, I can't get upset?"

No response.

Things couldn't get worse.

They got worse.

"Mike," my wife called from the other side of the house. "Can you do me a favor?"

I thought about my answer long and hard. Half a second later, I said, "No, I can't."

Some people say that if two individuals stare into each other's eyes for eight seconds or more without moving, they're going to either kiss or kill one another. My wife and I didn't kiss. After our eight-second stare, she threw down the gauntlet, challenging me to prove that I care about her needs and not just my own. Of course, this dilemma was bound to come up. I'd done something long ago to cause it. At the altar, I'd said, *I do.*

"I care about your needs," I said in my own defense. "I just have nothing else to give right now. This medicine is making me nuts. I'm wiped out and I'm drained."

Clearly I was dramatic as well.

I retreated from what was slowly becoming a death match. My son tried to help.

"Daddy, maybe you should just take a cool bath and cool off."

When I told my son it wouldn't work, he asked if he could take a bath. He likes to take long baths because his skin shrivels up. He says the wrinkles make him look older, and he wants to look older. I told him that "older" isn't better. "Older" means more problems.

"Trust me," I said. "Stay young — take a short bath."

My wife walked by and didn't say a word — the silent treatment. She called her parents and learned they both had the flu. She asked if they needed her help. Evidently they didn't because she kept insisting that they did.

When she got off the phone, she asked if I was going to say sorry. Typical guy, I said, "Sorry for what?"

She didn't say a word. She got back on the phone, this time with her sister, and she learned her sister was helping their parents with shopping and cooking while they were sick. My wife started crying.

"Why do you get to help and I don't?" she asked her sister.

When that phone call ended, I went to my wife and said I was sorry for what I'd done. I asked if she felt OK. Things were bad for my wife, too. I didn't have to make matters worse.

Matters got even worse. My wife reamed me for leaving our son in the bath too long—he was all shriveled up. With my medicine making me more and more anxious and insensitive, I struck back at my wife, saying her parents didn't want her help because her help always creates more work.

Oooops!

About an hour later, the house was quiet and still. My wife was in the bedroom avoiding me for what I'd said. I was in the living room avoiding responsibility for what I'd said. Our son tried to help. He turned on the TV looking for something to cheer everyone up. He found news about the earthquakes and tsunamis in Japan. Not a cheerful piece of TV, but we all came together to watch.

Yes, things could be a lot worse. My wife and I hadn't killed each other. We never were going to kill each other. We apologized and made up—like we usually do. Japan's epic problems made our simple domestic issues look like grains of sand, nothing to complain about.

A few days later, I cut my head open at work. (I'm really not making this up.) While the doctor punched staples into my skull, I smiled, ignoring the pain. "Things could be a lot worse," I said calmly.

Who am I kidding? I was furious. "God," I yelled. "It just keeps getting better and better."

Maybe we never learn.

— March 2011

About the Author

MICHAEL PICARELLA HAS BEEN WRITING HIS FAMILY humor column, *Family Men Don't Wear Name Brands*, for The Acorn Newspapers since 2006. He was a newspaper reporter and features writer for more than six years, he worked as a marketing writer and director at Nappic Communications for several more years, creating, among many other successful marketing campaigns, a series of viral ads that was inducted into MarketingSherpa's Viral Hall of Fame, and he's the writer-director behind the two highly unknown independent movies, *1 2 3* and *Punchcard Player*. Picarella paid a lot of money for his BFA from the Academy of Art University in San Francisco and he relocated to Los Angeles to make movies. Today, he still lives in Los Angeles, with his wife, son, pet beagle and no more movies to his name (but still working on it). To read other stories, please visit www.MichaelPicarellaColumn.com.

About the Illustrator

F.M. HANSEN'S CARTOONS HAVE BEEN PUBLISHED IN numerous anthologies worldwide, and his artwork is displayed in several galleries, including Gallery Nucleus in Alhambra, CA; WMA Gallery in Culver City, CA; Red Gate Gallery in London and several other fine institutions you'll probably never set foot in. He's currently at work on an animated comic strip and on several cartoon projects for clients near and far from Los Angeles, where he lives with his wife, daughter and their smelly dog, Snowball. To see more of Hansen's work, please visit www.fmhansen.com.

www.ingramcontent.com/pod-product-compliance
Lightning Source LLC
Chambersburg PA
CBHW031126090426
42738CB00008B/988